TRAVEL AND LEARN

THE NEW GUIDE TO EDUCATIONAL TRAVEL

by Evelyn Kaye

BLUE PENGUIN PUBLICATIONS
LEONIA NJ

TRAVEL AND LEARN

Published by
Blue Penguin Publications
147 Sylvan Avenue
Leonia NJ 07605 USA

Every effort has been made to ensure the accuracy of the information in this book, but the world of travel is subject to constant change. The publishers take no responsibility for inaccuracies relating to the material included. Readers are urged to contact the organizations directly before making travel plans.

Printed in the United States of America.

Library of Congress Catalog Card Number 90-81540

ISBN 0-9626231-0-5

CONTENTS

THE AUTHOR

EVELYN KAYE has traveled extensively on her own and with educational travel groups. She is the author of several books including *The Family Guide to Cape Cod; Crosscurrents: Children, Families and Religion; College Bound: The Students Handbook to Getting Ready, Moving In and Succeeding on Campus*; and *How to Treat TV with TLC.*

Her articles have appeared in major magazines and newspapers including *Travel & Leisure, Adventure Travel, McCalls, Parents, New York* and *Glamour,* and in the *New York Times, NJ Record, Boston Globe, Boston Herald,* and *Manchester Guardian.*

She has served as President of the American Society of Journalists and Authors, the leading organization of nonfiction writers in the United States, on the Executive Council, and as Director of the ASJA Annual Writers' Conference in New York.

INTRODUCTION

Francis Bacon (1561-1626)

Travel, in the younger sort, is a part of education; in the elder, a part of experience.

INTRODUCTION

I'm a traveler with severe travelitis. As soon as the possibility of a trip comes up, my immediate reaction is: "Great! When can I start packing?"

Over the years, I've learned to fit everything I need into a carry-on bag; bring enough film for my camera; not worry if I forget my comb; and mutter my soothing mantra, "I Am Mellow as Jell-o" to cope with crises.

I've been lucky enough to visit hundreds of places. I've toured California, New England, Texas, Arkansas, Illinois, Wisconsin, Alabama, Virginia, Colorado, the Florida Keys, the bayous of Louisiana and the Grand Canyon. And I've traveled in England, Scotland, Ireland and Wales, France, Italy, Switzerland, Denmark, Holland and Belgium, Australia and New Zealand, India, Israel, Ecuador, Mexico and Canada.

But the longer I travel, the more I longed to find a book like this, a book that puts together trips offering more than just a vacation. I enjoy discovering the stories about the places I visit. I want to know more about the countries I tour. I like meeting experts who can take me to interesting sights off the beaten track. And I love learning the words and phrases of a new language.

But I could never find the right book. So I decided I would have to write it myself.

This new kind of travel book is designed to meet the needs of a new breed of traveler. It's for those who want to learn as they roam and like to expand their horizons and find new challenges. It's for the woman who takes off for a bicycle tour of China though she hasn't pedalled a bike since high school, or for the man who signs up for a college course in Tibetan mythology because the topic fascinates him. It's for the active couple who decide to spend a vacation assisting an ecology research project in California, or for the retired accountant who longs to spend a month in Madrid to learn Spanish.

All these experiences are possible because today education and travel have become inextricably linked.

In the old-style travel books I've read, there's a distinct feeling that it's a sign of weakness to travel with a group; the authors project the image of organized chaos you remember from the movie, *If This Is Tuesday, It Must Be Belgium*. It's an article of faith that True Travelers wander about alone, peer at the major sights which they try to find unaided, struggle to choose a room, a meal, a bath, and never admit they don't know what's going on. You are supposed to be strong enough to do it on your own.

But those of us who have been out there on the travel circuit know that much of traveling today is just like being at home. You spend too much time doing things you hoped to avoid. Too many airports look alike, too many hotels have American names, and too many restaurants offer fast-food service. What's more, it's never been much fun trying to find a room at midnight in a strange city with no place to cash a check and where no one speaks your language.

The new breed of travelers prepares for what's coming up, wants someone else to choose places to sleep and eat, and likes to be guided on the trip by an expert who'll know what's the best thing to do. In fact she or he travels just like the authors of the old-style guidebooks have always done—travel with a local expert who knows where to go and what to see.

Mark Twain once wrote:

> "Travel is fatal to prejudice, bigotry and narrow-mindedness, all foes to real understanding. Likewise tolerance, or broad, wholesome, charitable views of men and things cannot be acquired by vegetating in our little corner of the earth all one's lifetime."

His words are as true today as when they were written. I have discovered that it can be enriching to join travel programs sponsored by a university or museum or educational organization, where the expertise and knowledge of a qualified leader expands your understanding and at the same time eliminates the hassles of everyday living so you can focus on the fascinating.

Today, educational travel has come into its own. The fastest growing segment of the travel and tourism field is the adult education vacation. But nothing happens overnight. What caused this change in American travel patterns?

BETTER EDUCATION. With more and more people completing high school and college, first-time travelers don't want a haphazard trip to a fascinating place. It's more fun to study the language and culture of a country or to take a seminar on art and architecture, or to listen to a scientist explain how volcanoes develop.

AN AGING POPULATION. A growing percentage of our population is over 40, so that today, older Americans outnumber the young. But American men and women between 40 and 70 enjoy better health, more energy, more money, and more leisure time than their parents ever did. They have an enthusiasm for travel but no longer want the hassles of bookings and tickets and arrangements. They may be widowed or divorced, or have a spouse who hates leaving home, so they prefer the companionship of a group tour with others who share their interest in bird-watching or studying Japanese.

MORE TRIPS, MORE CHOICES. A few years ago, only a handful of organizations offered learning vacations. Today the list keeps growing—from colleges that run seminars to the craft museum that tours potters' studios to the wilderness organization that leads trips to nature preserves to the

Smithsonian Institution which offers its Associates more than 160 programs every year.

You will find hundreds of universities and colleges offer educational travel to students, alumni, and associates. Most trips are open to everyone although if you're not a student, you may have to pay a fee to become a member or an associate. Sometimes there are reading lists and a written paper to be submitted when you complete the program, and you can earn academic credits.

Some institutions use professional travel agencies that specialize in educational tours led by experts who give seminars and lectures along the way. And some trips can take you to places the average traveler doesn't see; a journey down the Nile River led by an Egyptian archaeologist, for example, visited tombs usually closed to the public.

The aim of this book is to offer you a selection of the best educational travel choices. I've interpreted the word 'educational' to include a broad range of learning experiences. The emphasis is academic, physical, artistic, and practical.

I've put together all the information about educational travel programs that I could find, to give you the broadest and most varied selection of choices. But I have not specified the organizations with which I've traveled, because your trip with them will not be the same as mine, and what you look for on your journeys reflects your interests and personality.

A journey is always unique and quite unpredictable, like falling in love. We travel with our individual views, expectations, and attitudes. We may travel to the same places but at different times and with different companions and under different circumstances. We experience different weather, different situations, different emotions. Every trip promises a taste of unique adventure, and the pleasant thrill of surprise.

Here's hoping you have wonderful journeys, and may your dreams come true.

HOW TO USE THIS BOOK

Isabella Bird (1831-1904)

Travellers are privileged to do the most improper things with perfect propriety.

HOW TO USE THIS BOOK

This book suggests a process of discovery for you. As you read, you can decide the kinds of educational travel experiences that interest you and then carefully choose the ones you'd like to take.

First, browse through the **Topics** section, looking at the range of options offered and picking out those activities and subjects you'd like to explore.

Second, turn to the **Organizations**, listed alphabetically, which describe the programs offered, and see if they mesh with what you'd like.

Third, write, call, or fax the organizations for brochures, itineraries, and details of the programs and make your decision.

Topics

This section describes the major program areas of educational vacations in this book—archaeology and history, the arts, with visits to museums and classes in painting and sculpture, and active outdoor courses in backpacking, trekking, hiking and biking. There are language and culture programs, several that focus on human relations, waterways, and programs on ecology, wildlife and more.

Organizations

The key section of the book provides the essential information for you to track down the trips which interest you.

All organizations have met the criteria I set and are designed to provide as wide a range of quality options as possible. The organizations were selected from mailings to hundreds of groups around the country. Every organization completed a questionnaire and supplied brochures and informational materials.

Those included in the book have:

- demonstrated strong educational programs;
- provided qualified leaders for trips and programs;
- been in business for a reasonable period of time;
- run successful trips before;
- provided helpful informational material;
- answered questions promptly;
- explained what prices include;
- welcomed inquiries;
- listed an office address and phone in the United States.

The organizations are listed alphabetically for easy reference, with the name, address, phone, fax number and contact person up front. That's followed by a description of their programs and information about their philosophy. Then there's an outline of what the price includes—some include roundtrip airfare, some don't—and a few sample trips to show the destinations, courses offered and the price range.

The next step is up to you: call, write, or fax them for more information. The organizations are ready to answer your questions and explain anything that sounds confusing. A responsible organization wants participants to gain the most benefit from its programs and is eager to help you make the right decision.

Definitions

The short descriptions include a variety of terms, which I've tried to use consistently. Here's what they mean.

Accommodations

It may be a luxury hotel, comfortable hotel, bargain hotel, university dorm, college room, houseboat, cruise ship, apartment, villa, cabin, hut, tent, or sleeping pad. The details are made clear in the printed materials you'll be sent, but check before you go. If you like a firm mattress or cannot sleep with street noise or have special needs, tell the organization in advance.

Meals

Take note of how many meals are provided. "Room and board" means all meals are included. If the words "board" or "meals" are not mentioned, check first, and be prepare to budget enough to buy food.
Some Meals usually includes breakfast and a few lunches or dinners, but the rest of the time you buy your own.
Most Meals means that you will only have to buy an occasional lunch or dinner and everything else is included.
All Meals means just what it says.

Airfare

When roundtrip airfare is included, it is usually calculated from the place the trip originates. You have to pay travel expenses to get to where the trip begins. If you're in New York, and the program starts in California, remember to include the cost of the cross-country trip.

When airfare is not included, the company usually makes arrangements for group fares through a travel agency. Check before you book your ticket.

Excursions, Tours

These refer to trips to places of interest lasting a day, a weekend, or longer. Before you sign up, you can ask the organization which places you will be visiting. If there are sights you are particularly interested in seeing, you can make sure there will be an opportunity to do so.

Transportation

Taking a bus, train, plane, and boat during the program is covered under transportation. It's a good idea to ask how much additional travel there will be, what additional costs may total, and details of what's involved. Besides, it's nice to know there'll be an elephant ride through the jungle or a jeep tour of the desert.

Permits, Fees

These cover entrance fees to museums, parks, castles, and sites of interest. You can ask for an estimate of the total cost of these items before you leave. Also ask if you should budget any money for tips.

Escorts, Guides, Leaders

The people who travel with the group are very important. Make sure you know who will be traveling with you, what their qualifications are, and how long they have been leading groups. This information is usually provided in the material about the trip. Most organizations carefully choose leaders and staff guides for their experience, knowledge, and abilities and are happy to give you the information.

College Credits

Many institutions offer educational credits for participation in travel study programs or courses. Because institutions have a variety of different criteria for awarding educational credits, you should contact the institution directly to find out its policy.

Special Note

The costs and the trip details listed are accurate at this writing, and will give you an idea of price and length of program. But travel experience has shown that no trip and no price is ever fixed in stone. All information and prices are subject to unexpected change. Please recognize that the costs quoted are *only guidelines* and *cannot be guaranteed.*

Take your time as you browse through the book and note those organizations which offer trips you might enjoy. Call or write for all the information you can, compare and contrast, as your high school English teacher used to say, and then make your decision.

This is the first edition of **TRAVEL AND LEARN**. I would be delighted to hear from those of you who go places and learn. Send me a letter about your experiences. Give me names of companies you can recommend. Let me know what was helpful to you, and what you'd like to have in the next edition. In the world of travel, things change from day to day. The information in this book is accurate as of March 1990.

My thanks to all those who completed questionnaires, sent materials, and took the time to check the accuracy of their listings. Special thanks to Janet Gardner and Dodi Schultz for their superb editorial help. And my admiration and thanks to my partner, Christopher Sarson, for his advice, assistance, patience and creativity as I wrote and we designed and produced the book in WordPerfect 5.0 on our computers.

Happy traveling!

Evelyn Kaye

TOPICS

Louise Arner Boyd (1887-1972)

Far north, hidden behind grim barriers of pack ice, are lands that hold one spellbound. Gigantic imaginary gates seem to guard these lands. The gates swing open, and one enters another world where men are insignificant amid the awesome immensity of lovely mountains, fiords, and glaciers.

TOPICS

You've decided to take an educational travel vacation. But what would you like to learn about? What kind of education are you looking for? And what kinds of programs are available today to those who want to travel and learn?

My interpretation of the word "education" is in its widest and most far-reaching sense. Learning takes place in classrooms, but true education can occur anywhere in the world with someone whose interest brings the subject alive.

An educational vacation includes the academic and intellectual. You can choose arts, sciences, literature, philosophy, economics, politics, education, or sociology. You can delight in the creative with painting, crafts, building, sculpture, design, illustration, writing, music, performances, or special events. You can enjoy hiking, rowing, rafting, paddling, climbing, swimming, dancing, skiing, snowshoeing, fishing, or riding. And you can try cooking, analyzing social problems, discussing politics, or reading philosophy. Take a chance: try something you've never studied before!

This section outlines your choices and what you can expect.

ARCHAEOLOGY AND HISTORY

Fascination with the past leads travelers to a variety of programs of study and exploration.

Crow Canyon in Colorado was once a thriving center with thousands of inhabitants who, for some reason, left their homes and abandoned the area. Today volunteers assist experienced researchers who are trying to discover what happened by examining the ruined buildings, tools and pottery shards left behind.

In Europe, there's a tour of sites important in the Second World War, led by a history professor. In Texas, you can join researchers exploring a recently discovered explosion-triggered crater of an ancient volcanic caldera, unusual in the region.

In Israel, travelers visit sites mentioned in the Bible, swim in the Sea of Galilee, and walk the narrow, cobbled streets of Jerusalem and Bethlehem. In Egypt, volunteers help excavate a 3300-year-old tomb in the desert, survey ancient irrigation systems, and sketch fragments of rediscovered pottery. In Turkey, a professor leads a tour of the earliest western civilizations. In France and Italy, volunteers can participate in programs restoring medieval buildings by helping to reconstruct stone and brick walls, paving, tiles and carvings.

In Belize, British Honduras, a program explores newly discovered mounds at Wild Cane Cay, believed to be one of major Maya trading sites in the area; long before the Europeans arrived, the Mayans traded pottery and copper and green obsidian. On Easter Island, 2000 miles off the coast of Chile, researchers are investigating the collapse of its society by excavating and screening materials from a site on the south shore.

Earthwatch lists several programs related to history and archaeology, including a project in England to search for remains of the Roman occupation along Hadrian's Wall, which took place about 138 A.D.; volunteers hunt for tools, coins, pottery, and other Roman artifacts, and excavate one of the stone forts that Hadrian's architects build on the Cumbrian coast.

Elderhostel programs include a large number of academic courses on history, archeology and geology at many university and college campuses.

ORGANIZATIONS OFFERING ARCHAEOLOGY AND HISTORY TRIPS:

American Jewish Congress
American Museum of Natural History
Canyonlands Field Institute
Crow Canyon Archeological Center
Denver Museum of Natural History
Earthwatch
Elderhostel
Foundation for Field Research
George Washington University
Humanities Institute
Interhostel
La Sabranenque
San Jose State University
Smithsonian
Stanford Alumni Association
Syracuse University
University of Wisconsin/Madison Outreach
University Research Expedition Program
University of California/Los Angeles
University Systems of Georgia

THE ARTS

You can spend a wonderful time traveling and learning about painting, sculpture, pottery, dance, theater, writing, music, photography, or crafts, for there are hundreds of programs on every aspect of the arts.

But are you a viewer or a doer? Viewers like to look, observe, browse, think, and consider the arts. Doers prefer to sketch a scene, learn the polka, practice the violin, or weave a hanging themselves.

For viewers, excursions and guided tours led by arts experts travel to see some of the great paintings and sculpture of the world. Cruises sail around South America visiting the art treasures of Argentina, Uruguay, and Brazil, including a 17th century monastery and the Palace of the Emperors in Rio de Janeiro. Lovers of Impressionist paintings can float down the canals in the south of France through scenery which inspired those glowing paintings of low bridges hung with ivy, picturesque villages, and yellow cornfields dotted with poppies. There are summer travel programs in France and Italy where you learn to see familiar paintings with new eyes.

Musicians can attend a bassoon camp or a chamber-music festival to enjoy harmonizing with others. Music lovers can travel with the Metropolitan Opera Guild to visit historic European cities and listen to superb concerts, operas, and recitals. For the active, there's a white-water rafting trip accompanied by a group that plays bluegrass music along the way.

Arts centers in Georgia, Arkansas, and Washington offer summer courses in writing, sketching, and crafts. Special museums take members on visits to Turkey's famous rug-weaving cities, or to Bali with its dances and festivals, or to the dramatic medieval art, architecture and paintings of Spain and Italy.

And there are literary experiences. You can hike amid the soaring mountains of Sedro Woolley, Washington as part of an outdoor seminar in poetry and prose readings about nature. You can attend writing workshops or courses in literature. And a most popular educational trip takes participants to live in a British university with theater performances, a trip to Stratford-upon-Avon, and seminars by eminent scholars on English literature, poetry, and drama.

ORGANIZATIONS OFFERING ARTS TRIPS:

Abercrombie & Kent
American Institute for Foreign Study
Arkansas Art Center
Arrowmont School
Art Institute of Chicago
Arts Abroad/School of Visual Arts
Augusta Heritage Center
Canyonlands Field Institute
Centrum Foundation
Chamber Music Festival
Consortium for International Education
Cornell's Adult University
Dillman's Creative Workshops
ECHO: The Wilderness Company
Edinboro at Oxford
Elderhostel
Folkways Institute/Travel
Glickman-Popkin Bassoon Camp
High Adventure Tours
Humanities Institute

Institute of China Studies
Interhostel
International Travel Study
Kentucky Institute for European Studies
Kosciuszko Foundation
Metropolitan Museum of Art
Metropolitan Opera Guild
National Registration Center for Study Abroad
Newark Museum
North Cascades Institute
Overseas Adventure Travel
Pacific Northwest Field Seminars
Parsons School of Design
Pratt Institute
Readers Theater
Rockland Community College/SUNY
San Jose State University
Smithsonian
Stanford Alumni Association
Syracuse University
Textile Museum
Toledo Museum of Art
University of California/Berkeley
University of California/Los Angeles
University of California/Santa Cruz
University of Detroit
University of Wisconsin/Madison
University of Wisconsin/Stevens Point
Western Illinois University
Ward Foundation
Western Michigan University
Wolf Trap Associates

BACKPACKING, TREKKING, HIKING, AND BIKING

"The backpack was heavy; my shoulders and hips hurt; trails were long and all gain; mosquitoes were abundant and hungry; when it wasn't raining it was hailing. So how do I feel about the Women's Beginner Backpack Trip? I loved it! I have come away from Yosemite feeling stronger and surer."

That's how a woman from California summed up her first experience of backpacking on a Sierra Club trip. The joys of exploring beautiful scenery entice thousands of people out into the mountains and hills to hike, trek, and backpack through national and state parks. Others enjoy the faster speed and greater freedom of a bike.

There are a wide variety of trips into national and state parks, wilderness areas, and attractive countryside for those ready to step out on foot or pedal their way around.

Hiking, sometimes called trekking, is steady walking along marked trails, wearing sturdy, comfortable footwear and carrying everything you need in a pack on your back. On day hikes, you take lunch, water, rain gear, and personal items for the day and spend the night at a base camp in a tent, or in a lodge, cabin or hotel.

Backpacking is more demanding; you carry everything you need with you, including camping equipment and food as well as clothes and personal needs. Some trips provide llamas, donkeys, mules, or sturdy local residents to carry the heavy gear, while you walk with a day pack.

Hiking introduces you to some of the most magnificent natural scenery in the world. You can visit the dozens of state and national parks in the United States including Yosemite, Yellowstone, Rocky Mountains, Adirondack, and many more. Or you can go abroad to hike through the Alps in Europe, visiting picturesque Swiss villages or French wine-growing towns. You can stroll along tree-shaded ramblers' paths in England, and stay in youth hostels. You can follow ancient Mayan trails in Peru, Chile, and Ecuador, trekking in the Andes to the hidden city of Machu Picchu.

Many established outdoor organizations specialize in hiking and are eager to help you set out for the first time. Most offer a range of trips for beginners, intermediates, and seasoned hikers. Some last for a weekend, a few days, or a week, while others last for several weeks or longer. You decide how much time you have, where you'd like to travel and how energetic you feel and then take off to discover the exhilaration of the natural world.

Biking trips speed through the countryside on side roads and winding lanes, with stops at interesting historical sites and special sites in different regions. Most bike trips are geared for different levels of expertise and provide a support van to carry those whose heart is willing but legs can't make the hills. On some bike trips, you camp out or stay in hostels; others offer comfortable hotels and gourmet meals along the way.

ORGANIZATIONS OFFERING BACKPACKING, TREKKING, HIKING, AND BIKING TRIPS:

Above-the-Clouds Trekking
Alaska Discovery
American Museum of Natural History
American Wilderness Experience
American Youth Hostels
Appalachian Mountain Club
Arctic Trek
Backroads Bicycle Touring
Baja Expeditions Inc.

Bighorn Expeditions
Camp Denali
Canyonlands Field Institute
Denver Museum of Natural History
Eye of the Whale
Gerhard's Bicycle Odysseys
Hugh Glass Backpacking Company
International Bicycle Tours
International Zoological Expeditions
Island Bicycle Adventures
Journeys International Inc.
Nantahala Outdoor Center
National Audubon Society
National Outdoor Leadership School
Nature Expeditions International
Outward Bound
Overseas Adventure Travel
Pacific Exploration Company
Pacific Northwest Field Seminars
Safariworld!
Sierra Club
Sobek
Stanford Alumni Association
Sun Valley Trekking Company
Texas Camel Corps at Witte Museum
University of Wisconsin/Stevens Point
Wild Horizons Expeditions
Wilderness Society
Wildlands Studies
Yellowstone Institute
Yosemite Mountaineering School

ECOLOGY

An ecological vacation involves you in the relationship between living organisms and their environment. If you are concerned about the environmental crisis and long to help in some way, an active experience may be the ideal choice.

Many of the organizations involved in environmental work are conscious of the need for observing the code of ecological behavior. Sobek Expeditions has designed a set of guidelines for those who take their trips, emphasizing the need to protect the natural resources of the regions through which they travel and respect for the communities there. The National Audubon Society created a statement of environmental behavior and guidelines which stress preservation and respect for nature. Other groups teach participants minimal-impact camping and meticulous waste removal in the wilderness. The National Parks Service has its own motto, "Take only photographs, leave only footprints," which has been adapted on water-bound trips to "Take only photographs, leave only bubbles."

To ease your conscience as you travel, look for groups with a strorg pro-environmental policy. And if you want to be actively involved, contact Earthwatch, the Foundation for Field Research, and the University Research Expedition Program, among others, where volunteers are welcomed on research projects.

You can work in the Mojave Desert of California to reconstruct a grassland basin which covered the desert millions of years ago and where mastodons, saber-toothed lions and other prehistoric animals once roamed. You can help researchers at the Barrier Islands Region of Virginia study how a pristine wetland functions, map the paths of wading birds and migrating shorebirds, count horseshoe crabs, and sort invertebrate prey. In Fairbanks, Alaska, you can work with a nutritionist and observe and monitor the different diets of captive musk oxen and caribou.

You can help to clear trails in national parks and forests. You can volunteer on a science project and study the behavior of dolphins and sea lions, feeding the animals and testing cognitive abilities as part of an environmental study. Farther afield, in India, you can assist researchers studying the behavior of Langur monkeys. In Mexico, volunteers help scientists count the birds in the cloud forest reserve of Tuxtla Guttierrez. And on the island of Corsica in the Mediterranean, you can work with marine biologists studying mating behavior in fish.

One volunteer, who worked in Fiji researching coral reefs commented: "Everybody wins—the investigators with funds and willing hands, the volunteers with grand adventure and a chance to help."

ORGANIZATIONS OFFERING ECOLOGICAL TRIPS:

Above the Clouds Trekking
Adventure Bound
Alaska Discovery
All-Outdoors Whitewater Trips
American Museum of Natural History
Appalachian Mountain Club
Arctic Treks
Arizona Raft Adventures
Camp Denali
Canyonlands Field Institute
Caretta Research Project
Cornell's Adult University
Crow Canyon Archeological Center
Denver Museum of Natural History

Earthwatch
ECHO: The Wilderness Company
Expeditions Inc.
Eye of the Whale
Field Guides
Foundation for Field Research
George Washington University
Heartwood Owner-Builder School
International Alpine School
International Zoological Expeditions
Island Bicycle Adventures
Journeys International
La Sabranenque Restoration Project
Marine Sciences Under Sail
Nantahala Outdoor Center
National Audubon Society
National Outdoor Leadership School
National Wildlife Federation
Nature Expeditions International
New York Botanical Gardens
North Cascades Institute
O.A.R.S.Inc
Our Developing World
Outward Bound
Overseas Adventure Travel
Pacific Northwest Field Seminars
Safariworld!
Sierra Club
Smithsonian
Sobek
Society Expeditions
Special Odysseys/Arctic
Sun Valley Trekking Company
University Research Expedition Program
Wilderness Society
Wildlands Studies
Wild Horizons Expeditions
World Wildlife Fund
Yellowstone Institute

HUMAN RELATIONS

For a first-hand educational experience, imagine living with a family in a foreign country, sharing their meals, learning their language, laughing at their jokes, and becoming part of their daily lives. You may be squeezed into a tiny room under the roof, be offered the only bed in the house, sleep under the stars in a tent or live in luxury in a spacious villa. You may find that dinner is not served until midnight. You may be offered onions for breakfast. You may never taste a decent cup of coffee.

These moments can prove to be the most memorable and educational parts of your stay abroad, even though they are not recognized by earned credits or academic achievement.

There are dozens of programs offering Americans the chance to learn more about how other people live. There are language programs, work programs, specialized skills programs, and exchange programs. You can live in Russia, Eastern Europe, or Asia. You can study in Scandinavian Folk Colleges. You can choose a home stay with families in Japan or China, Brazil or Argentina, Ghana or Zimbabwe, among dozens of others.

Some programs last a few weeks or a few months. Others offer semesters abroad, or even a full year in another country. Sometimes you need to study the language. Other times, your assistance is welcomed, even if you can't say a word.

You'll find archaeological and reconstruction programs with active physical involvement. There are tours emphasizing social and political issues, so that you meet teachers, farmers, business people and politicians. There are language programs where you are absorbed into the community and see your own country from a totally new perspective.

If learning more about other people is your goal, choose a program that gives you the opportunity to experience the fascination of a different culture, a new language, and a change in your lifestyle.

ORGANIZATIONS OFFERING HUMAN RELATIONS TRIPS:

AFS Intercultural Programs
American Institute for Foreign Study
American Jewish Congress
Consortium for International Education
Council for International Education
Council on International Educational Exchange
Edinboro at Oxford Experience
Elderhostel
Experiment in International Living
Folkways Institute/Travel
Foundation for American-Chinese Cultural Exchange
French-American Exchange
High Adventure Tours
Humanities Institute
Interhostel
International Council for Cultural Exchange
International Travel Study
Journeys International
Kentucky Institute for European Studies
Kosciuszko Foundation
La Sabranenque
Los Angeles Community College
North Cascades Institute
Our Developing World
Outward Bound
People to People International
San Francisco State University
San Jose State University

Scandinavian Seminar
Smithsonian
Sobek
Smithsonian
Stanford Alumni Association
State University of New York/New Paltz
State University of New York/Rockland
Syracuse University
Towson State University
Tulane University
United States-China Peoples Friendship Association
United States-Japan Cross Culture Center
University of California/Berkeley
University of California/Los Angeles
University of New OrleansUniversity of Rhode Island
University of Southwestern Louisiana
University of Wisconsin/Madison
University of Wisconsin/Stevens Point
University Studies Abroad Consortium
University System of Georgia
Volunteers for Peace
Western Michigan University
Western Washington University

LANGUAGE AND CULTURE

Bon jour!
Guten tag!
Buenos dias!
Shalom!
Sayonara!

The fascination of a new language is that it offers a window into another world. You not only learn words for "student," "umbrella," and firehouse," but you are introduced to a new culture and another lifestyle through the language.

Eskimos have hundreds of words for snow, the Greeks have a vast vocabulary for the varieties of love, and the French and Italians have so many words related to food that they are recognized as international. A "croissant"is always a "croissant" and "spaghetti" needs no translation. You'll also find that "blue jeans" and "hamburgers" are now internationally recognized.

The most challenging and effective way to study a foreign language is to go to the country where it's spoken, and immerse yourself in the daily life. Somehow when you have to buy bread and no one speaks English, you'll learn what to request very quickly. And if you're hopelessly lost, you'll find out how to ask directions.

At first, you won't even be able to fathom the bus schedule or find your way along unfamiliar streets. But as the days pass, you can find your way around, the language begins to sound quite normal, the people who looked alike turn into individuals, and your perspective moves from a critical comparison of what they're doing wrong to an open-minded appreciation of the differences.

The dozens of universities, colleges, and educational groups who organize language courses abroad expect that you will make a serious commitment to daily study and homework in order to gain the most benefit from the experience.

A typical day begins with breakfast in the college cafeteria, or in the hotel or pension or with your host family. Then you walk or bus to the school where classes usually start about eight or nine in the morning. Most courses offer four or five hours of instruction covering vocabulary, grammar, conversation, and pronunciation. Teachers are usually residents of the country and try to speak as little English as possible. On the first day, students take a test to determine their level of ability. Classes are kept small and the pace is adapted to the group's abilities. There's usually a short mid-morning break.

When classes end, you may lunch at the school or with your host family, or on your own. There will be time during the day to study in the language labs using headphones and tapes, attend lectures on the culture and history of the country, or take extra classes. You will also have homework to prepare for the next day. Although there will be temptations to skip some of the work, your teachers will emphasize that in order to gain fluency in a new language, you should study and speak it as much as you can for the time you are there.

Language programs range from the simple to the luxurious. You may stay in a college dorms, in a hotel, in a rented room, a palazzo by the ocean, an old castle, or live with a local family. Some programs offer a tour of the country as well as excursions to places of interest.

So what would you like to learn?

In Mexico, there are dozens of Spanish-language schools, many of them in Cuernavaca, a center of Spanish language instruction. In Guatemala, you can study not only Spanish but Mam and Quiche, indigenous regional languages. In Spain, there are language courses in Seville, Madrid, Salamanca, Ovideo and Pamplona, among others.

You can learn French in Quebec, Canada, or cross the Atlantic to France to learn how they speak it in Paris, Besancon, Montpellier, Nimes, or Toulon, in the Pyrenees, in Normandy and on the French Riviera among others.

There are German classes in Innsbruck, Hamburg, Tuebinger, and Kassel. In Vienna, there's a language course and seminar on concerts and musical performances. In Cracow, Lublin, and Warsaw you can study Polish. In Israel, there are Ulpan courses where new immigrants and visiting foreigners take intensive courses in Hebrew. In Rio de Janeiro, Brazil, you can study Portuguese.

In Italy, you can study Italian in the medieval village of Poppi, or in Bologna, Turin, or Florence. Or you can go to the charming seaside resort of Viareggio, where students live in a villa close to the beach.

The majority of courses focus on learning European languages. But for those who appreciate the growing importance of the Pacific Rim countries, there are some opportunities to learn Japanese and Chinese. Shanghai University offers a summer program of Chinese followed by a tour of the country. Other groups offer home-stays and Japanese-language programs in Tokyo. One university offers a trip to Inner Mongolia for an intensive eight weeks course in Chinese language and culture.

A Scandinavian program invites students of all ages, including Elderhostel participants, to live and study Swedish in Folk Colleges. There are also cooking (and eating) courses in China, Italy, and France taught by experts in the kitchen, where you'll absorb a useful culinary vocabulary as well as delicious meals.

Several programs for high-school students arrange for young people to spend the summer or a full year abroad living with a family in Australia, France, Italy, England, Spain, China, Japan, or Russia among other countries.

ORGANIZATIONS OFFERING LANGUAGE AND CULTURE PROGRAMS:

AFS Intercultural Programs
American Institute for Foreign Study
Casa Xelaju De Espanol/Guatemala
Centro di Cultura Italian Casentino
Compton Community College
Consortium for International Education
Council on International Educational Exchange
Cuauhnahuac-Mexico
Elderhostel
Europa-Kolleg Kassel/Germany
Experiment in International Living
Folkways Institute
Foundation for American-Chinese Cultural Exchanges
French-American Exchange
Hazan Master Classes in Italian Cooking
Institute of China Studies
Interhostel
International Council for Cultural Exchange
International Travel Study
Kentucky Institute for European Studies
Kibbutz Aliya Desk
Kosciuszko Foundation
La Varenne Cooking School/France
Language Studies Enrollment Center
Los Angeles Community College
Metropolitan State College
National Registration Center for Study Abroad
North Carolina Central University
Rockland Community College/SUNY
San Francisco State University
San Jose State University
Scandinavian Seminar
State University of New York/New Paltz
Syracuse University
Towson State University
Tulane University
United States-China Peoples Friendship Association
United States-Japan Cross Culture Center
University of California/Berkeley
University of New Orleans
University of Rhode Island

University of Southwestern Louisiana
University of Wisconsin/Stevens Point
University Studies Abroad Consortium
University System of Georgia
Western Washington University

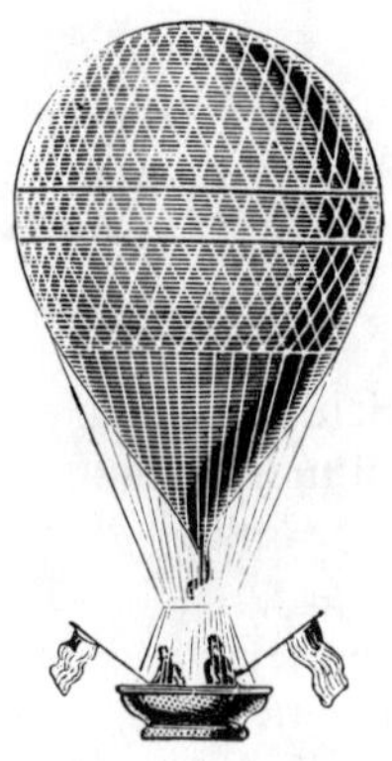

WATERWAYS

About two-thirds of our planet Earth is covered with water. To learn more about streams, rivers, lakes, and oceans, educational trips afloat can provide a new perspective on land-bound lives.

Perhaps you'd enjoy river-rafting down a white-water stream in America, Chile, Costa Rica, Peru, India, China, Australia, or New Zealand.

Today's modern rubber rafts keep afloat on the tossing waves and drift gently along on the river current between high canyon walls, low hills, or sandy shores edged with green trees, bushes and unusual plants. You'll see fantastic vistas, night skies sparkling with stars, and enjoy a new view of the world from the water. Most companies offer a choice of a large raft powered by motor or oars, smaller rafts for about eight people where the group paddles, or rafts or kayaks for one or two people. There are also raft schools which teach river-rafting skills to would-be guides.

A visit to Alaska often includes wilderness trips by canoe, sea kayak or cruise ship. One canoe excursion paddles through Admiralty Island National Monument Wilderness, where there are more brown bears and bald eagles than people. Or you can kayak on the Alaskan fjords or Glacier Bay, or alongside Hubbard Glacier. Fishing trips and photography seminars are popular.

In warmer waters, there are sea-kayak trips to Belize in Central America, where you paddle around the Barrier Reef, camp on deserted sandy beaches, drink milk from coconuts freshly fallen from the palm trees, and dive for shellfish for dinner. Or you can explore the islands of Baja California. Down Under in Australia, there's a sea-kayak exploration of the Great Barrier Reef to admire the coral shoals and vividly colored fish.

For those who prefer comfort, cruise ships provide civilization with a little rocking on the waves. Elegant vessels offer gourmet meals, air conditioning, and clean sheets as they travel through Alaska, the Arctic or the Antarctic, around the cities of the Mediterranean, up the Amazon and Orinoco Rivers of South America, up the Yangtze River in China, or along the romantic Danube in Europe. Most cruises carry experts aboard who present lectures, films and informational seminars about the region. Some cruises offer swimming pools, aerobics, and jogging tracks as well, and can last a week, a month, or even several months. One canal-boat cruise down the canals of France provides a grand piano aboard.

For would-be sailors, sailing schools offer vacations that promise to teach you the essential skills in a week in the waters of the Caribbean, Florida, or New York.

ORGANIZATIONS OFFERING TRIPS ON THE WATER:

Abercrombie & Kent International
Adventure Bound
Alaska Discovery
All-Outdoors Whitewater Trips
American Museum of Natural History
American Wilderness Experience
Annapolis Sailing School
Appalachian Mountain Club
Arctic Trek
Arizona Raft Adventures
Baja Expeditions
Bighorn Expeditions
Camp Denali
Denver Museum of Natural History

ECHO: The Wilderness Company
Expeditions Inc.
Eye of the Whale
Foundation for Field Research
Hugh Glass Backpacking Company
Journeys International
Los Angeles Community College
Marine Sciences Under Sail
Metropolitan Museum of Art
Nantahala Outdoor Center
National Audubon Society
National Outdoor Leadership School
Nature Expeditions International
New York Botanical Gardens
O.A.R.S.Inc
Offshore Sailing School
Outward Bound
Overseas Adventure Travel
Pacific Exploration Company
Sierra Club
Slickrock Adventures
Smithsonian
Sobek
Society Expeditions
Special Odysseys/Arctic
Stanford Alumni Association
Texas Camel Corps at Witte Museum
VIP Travel
Western River Expeditions
Wilderness Society
World Wildlife Fund
Yellowstone Institute

WILDLIFE

The world of animals is shrinking. More and more species are becoming extinct, disappearing forever from the face of the earth. Well-meaning efforts to save animals in captivity may destroy their ability to survive in the wild life for which they are designed.

But there is still some pristine wilderness left where animals roam free as they once did centuries ago. You will find wonderful educational travel experiences that focus on animals and the environment, led by qualified naturalists and regional experts.

In Africa, you can visit the Serengeti National Park with 5600 square miles of wilderness alive with lions, leopards, hyenas, cheetahs, giraffes and more. Every year the wildebeest and zebras migrate across the plains, an unforgettable sight of millions of animals in vast herds searching for new grasslands. In Tanzania's Ngorongoro Crater, a 2000-foot-deep natural amphitheater formed by the collapse of an extinct volcano, you can see thousands of gazelles, hyenas, lions, elephants, and pink flamingoes.

In Kenya's Samburu Game Reserve, there are rhinoceros, buffaloes, elephants, oryxes, giraffes and rare species not often seen in the wild like the Somali ostrich, vulturine guinea fowl, and the leopard. In Rwanda, you may find mountain gorillas, the last of these shy, rare, and wonderful animals, living among the trees and scrub of the Akagera National Park. Or you may spot hippos and crocodiles as your boat rides through the reed-filled waterways of the park.

In Australia, there are kangaroos and wallabies leaping through the outback and buffaloes, wild horses, and unusual birds in Kakadu National Park near Darwin.

In Nepal's Chitwan National Park, you can ride an elephant and look for the Royal Bengal tiger, the one-horned rhino, spotted deer, wild boars, monkeys and leopards in the jungle. And in Ecuador's Galapagos Islands, you can see huge tortoises a century old, blue-footed boobies on nests with their fluffy offspring, penguins, fur seals, playful sea lions, marine iguanas, pelicans, frigate birds, and swallow-tailed gulls.

If you want a hands-on experience, you can travel to St. Croix, in the U.S. Virgin Islands, where the Turtle Project uses satellite tracking and harnesses to observe the movements of sea turtles. In Vietnam, volunteers work to save the lives and habitat of Eastern sarus cranes, the tallest flying birds in the world.

In North Carolina, researchers study the effects of the forest sanctuaries for black bears established in 1971. In Sarasota, Florida, studies of dolphins focus on their social interactions. In Costa Rica, there's a project to study howler monkeys, while in Liberia, volunteers help research the distribution of chimpanzees in the tropical rain forests.

ORGANIZATIONS OFFERING WILDLIFE TRIPS:

Abercrombie & Kent International
Alaska Discovery
American Museum of Natural History
American Wilderness Experience
Appalachian Mountain Club
Baja Expeditions Inc.
Canyonlands Field Institute
Caretta Research Project
Cornell's Adult University
Denver Museum of Natural History

Earthwatch
Eye of the Whale
Field Guides
Foundation for Field Research
Heritage Institute
Hugh Glass Backpacking Company
International Zoological Expeditions
Island Bicycle Adventures
Journeys International
Marine Sciences Under Sail
National Audubon Society
National Wildlife Federation
Nature Expeditions International
North Cascades Institute
Overseas Adventure Travel
Pacific Exploration Company
Pacific Northwest Field Seminars
Safariworld!
San Jose State University
Sierra Club
Slickrock Adventures
Smithsonian
Sobek
Society Expeditions
Special Odysseys/Arctic
Stanford Alumni Association
Texas Camel Corps at Witte Museum
University of California/Los Angeles
University of Wisconsin/Stevens Point
University Research Expedition Program
VIP Travel
Wilderness Society
Wild Horizons Expeditions
Wildlands Studies
World Wildlife Fund
Yellowstone Institute

WHALE WATCHING

"A night sky with stars arching to eternity; the tide rolling in, inexorably, as our skiff moves slowly around the sparkling San Ignacio Lagoon. We pause, watch gray whale backs circle closer. The crewman helming the skiff guns the motor, producing a gush of bubbles.

"Astern a whale blows under water; the whale's bubbles rise to the surface like an answer. The crewman says he likes to think he and the whale are talking together.

"Suddenly a huge head rises quietly and rests lightly on the side of the skiff. Nobody moves. Then the silence of awe is broken; those nearest reach out to touch and to stroke, carefully avoiding the intelligent, alien eye, commenting with quiet excitement on the texture and feel of the skin, without fear."

That was the experience of a woman from Reno, Nevada on her first whale-watching adventure. You can find whales in coastal waters around the United States, traveling thousands of miles during migration to reach the Alaska and California coasts, spouting water or breaching as they erupt into the air with an awe-inspiring swoop of their huge bulk. The largest of all, the blue whale, is up to 100 feet long and can weigh 150 tons.

But years of commercial whaling have steadily decreased the whale population. Today, international efforts struggle to protect the remaining animals, but fewer and fewer seem to survive each year.

Those who have seen live whales in their natural habitat are affected by the experience. I still remember when I saw one rising out of the water, and then heard through a microphone aboard the strange whining and singing of a whale under water a few hundred feet away from our boat near Hawaii.

If you long to see a real whale, don't wait too long, or, sadly, they may be gone.

ORGANIZATIONS OFFERING WHALE-WATCHING TRIPS:

American Wilderness Experience
Baja Expeditions Inc.
National Audubon Society
Nature Expeditions International
Sierra Club
Slickrock Adventures
Smithsonian
Sobek
VIP Travel
World Wildlife Fund

"There's something about their enormousness that draws us. We wonder at the mystery of where they go, what they eat, how they communicate and navigate. We wonder what it's like to live in a gravityless environment where sounds make up most of the way you see." noted a natural history teacher from Seattle.

ORGANIZATIONS

The following carefully selected list of organizations represents those that met the criteria for this book, chosen for their experience, reliability and quality of educational programs. They are listed alphabetically for easy reference, and offer a wide range of educational travel study programs in the United States and around the world.

Alexandra David-Neel(1868-1969)

Travel not only stirs the blood, it also gives strength to the spirit."

ABERCROMBIE & KENT

Address: **1420 Kensington Road, Suite 103**
Oak Brook IL 60521
Phone: **(708)954-2944**
Fax: **(708)954-3324**
Contact: **Helga Sommer Westell**

The name Abercrombie & Kent symbolizes comfort and style, as it has since the company began in 1962. Today its escorted tours, limited to 18 passengers, travel to Africa, Australia, New Zealand, Papua New Guinea, the Orient, Egypt, India, and Europe and enjoy safaris, cruises along the canals of France, visits to elegant English country houses, and more.

Directors Jorie and Geoffrey Kent assert: "Wherever you travel, your Abercrombie & Kent itinerary is simply the best way to travel. We confirm the commitment which has set us apart from other tour planners: to provide personal service for our travellers. Hotels, meals and transportation are all the best, and all add immeasurably to your comfort."

In Africa, participants view the country from an amphibian plane which flies low over the terrain or speeds across lakes and ocean. An Egyptian trip flies from Cairo south down the Nile river with stops at the pyramids, Khartoum, and other places of historic interest.

Tours in Russia take travelers from Moscow to Leningrad aboard a comfortable private train, built for official use in 1983. In France, travelers relax aboard the luxury canal barge, *Fleur de Lys* with swimming pool, grand piano, and canopied four-poster beds, as it explores the Alsace region.

In Papua New Guinea, there are visits to the Huli Wigmen of Tari Valley and to the tribes along the Sepik River basin, as well as a tour of the vast orchid collection of Lae's Botanical Gardens and Aseki, home of the once-feared warriors, the Kukukuku. The tour ends with a week in New Zealand.

Price includes:

Accommodations, meals, transfers, transportation, and escorts. Airfare not included although flights can be booked through the company.

Sample trips:

$5,720 for six day train ride in Russia.
$7,280 for 26 days in Papua New Guinea.
$8,000 for 14 days flying over Africa's Rift Valley.
$26,000 for six nights on *Fleur de Lys* barge in France.

ABOVE THE CLOUDS TREKKING

Address: **PO Box 398**
Worcester MA 01602-0398
Phone: **(508)799-4499/(800)233-4499**
Fax: **(508)797-4779**
Contact: **Steve Conlon, Director**

"By traveling in small groups, in the same style as the local people, we are treated not as tourists but as fellow human beings. We are often invited into the homes of the local people. By the time the trip is finished, our goal is that you have had the experience of climbing inside the heart and mind of the native population, and gained some sense, some insight, into what the world looks and feels like from inside the windows of the villages we pass," notes Director Steve Conlon.

Treks through Nepal and the Himalayas and safaris and treks in Kenya, Madagascar and Zaire, and in the Andes of Peru and Ecuador are the company's most popular trips. The majority of participants are between the ages of 35 and 55.

The trip to Machu Picchu avoids the standard Inca Trail and follows the route the Incas took to hide from the Spanish in the remote Vilcabamba region. In East Africa, there are visits to the less well-known national parks of Chizarira, Chobe, and Moremi/Okavango Delta, as well as to Victoria Falls. In Nepal, there's a hike along the Jaljale Himal High Ridge, opened in 1988, with views of Everest and Kangchenjunga along the way. And in Europe, there's hiking amid Yugoslavia's Julian Alps, with overnight stops in mountain huts.

Price includes:

Accommodations, all meals, services of guides, cooks and porters, transfers, transportation, permits, entrance fees, camping equipment.

Sample trips:

$1,950 for 23 days in Peru.
$1,975 for 30 days on Jaljale Himal High Ridge, Nepal.
$2,900 for 15 days in North Yemen.
$3,200 for 22 days in East Africa.

"Your trip was wonderful in every way," reported one traveler after her visit to Nepal. "The trek was perfect. The food was delicious, the equipment worked perfectly, and the route was well-planned. Not only was our guide very knowledgeable about the country, but he is a skilled photographer willing to share his talent with others."

ADVENTURE BOUND INC.

Address: 2932 H Road
Grand Junction CO 81505
Phone: (303)241-5633/800)423-4668
Fax: (303)243-2767
Contact: Tom Kleinschnitz

With 20 years of river rafting experience, Adventure Bound offers trips through some of the most beautiful scenery in the West, designed for both beginners and more experienced rafters. One participant has taken annual trips with the company for 14 years - first with his children, now with his grandchildren.

The choice is wide: two to five days of rafting down a variety of rivers. There's Westwater Canyon on the Colorado river, or a trip on the Green River through Dinosaur National Monument, or down the Yampa River, one of the last untouched major wild rivers which swells with spring run-off. More challenging rapids are found in Cataract Canyon. On the upper Green River the boats pass through the magnificent scenery of Desolation and Gray Canyons.

For those who want to spend more time on the river, ask about the 18-day trip that follows the route John Wesley Powell took a hundred years ago when he first explored the Colorado River and paddled through the Grand Canyon.

Participants travel in neoprene rafts with oars, paddles, or motors. There are inflatable canoes and paddle boats for those who want to try paddling on their own along the way.

Price includes:

Camping accommodations, all meals on the river, transportation to put-in point and return to hotel, equipment, guides.

Sample trips:

$210 for two days on Westwater Canyon, Colorado.
$407 for four days on the Yampa river, Colorado,
$525 for five days on Green River Wilderness, Utah.

AFS INTERCULTURAL PROGRAMS

Address: 313 East 43rd Street
New York, NY 10017
Phone: (212)949-4242
Fax: (212)949-9379
Contact: Scott D. Ramey

The American Field Service has a motto, "Walk together, talk together, all ye peoples of the earth; then and only then shall ye have peace."

Its long history of promoting understanding between nations began in 1914 and led to the first AFS intercultural programs in 1947. It is the leading international exchange organization worldwide and is a founding member of the Council on Standards for International Travel. More than 170,000 students and host families have participated in its programs.

Today, AFS programs involve 55 countries in Europe, the United States and Canada, South America, Central America, Africa, Asia, the Pacific, the Middle East, and the Caribbean. A Connecticut parent who hosted a student from abroad said: "I believe these programs give average Americans a rare chance to promote international good will, cooperation, and cultural understanding on a very fundamental level."

The AFS sends American high-school students between the ages of 15 and 19 to live abroad with host families. It also brings foreign students to live with American families. Other exchanges involve secondary-school teachers. Students stay for a year, a semester or six to eight weeks in the summer.

One teenager from Pennsylvania who lived in Uruguay wrote: "To me, the world is no longer divided, no longer made up of Americans, Russians, Uruguayans, Africans, and Japanese. It is made up of people, all with thoughts, hopes, ideas, and dreams. We have different cultures, but we are all people."

Most American host families have positive reactions. "We heard there are all kinds of experiences between host families and exchange students, but we didn't believe it could be so perfect," enthused one family in Massachusetts.

Another wrote: "A young man from Chile stepped off the bus, and another chapter in our lives began. If someone told me that a family could fall in love with a total stranger in four days, I would say 'Impossible.' But it happened."

Price includes:

Airfare, accommodations, all meals, transportation, excursions, instruction.

Sample trips:

$2,750 for six to eight weeks home stays in Europe, Middle East, Asia.
$3,000 for eight weeks home stay/language course in Japan, Europe, Turkey.
$3,950 for six months in Latin America.
$4,900 for 11 months in Asia, South Pacific, Middle East, Europe, USSR, Latin America.

ALASKA DISCOVERY

Address: **369 South Franklin**
Juneau AK 99801
Phone: **(907)586-1911**
Contact: **Bethany Berman**

Alaska Discovery was honored by the Alaska state legislature for providing "absolute minimum impact on flora and fauna combined with maximum visitor appreciation" in its kayak explorations of Glacier Bay and other remote areas in southeast Alaska.

Its philosophy emphasizes that "our need for, and use of, the wilderness should not conflict with the same needs and uses of this land by its present inhabitants. We hope that each of our guests will discover the joy of slipping quietly, unnoticed, through the Alaska wilderness."

From June to September, there are dozens of trips offered including kayak touring in Glacier Bay National Park, visits to Hubbard Glacier and Russell Fiord Wilderness Area, canoeing and fishing in the Admiralty Island Wilderness Area, river rafting on the Yukon to the Gulf of Alaska, a special photo expedition, and explorations from a wilderness lodge base camp.

You don't need boating experience, but good physical condition and excellent general health are recommended for touring Alaska's back country. Trips last from four to ten days, and can be combined to gain a fuller experience of the region.

Price includes:

Accommodations, all meals, transportation, camping gear, equipment, floatplane, park fees. Sleeping bags and rain gear available for rent.

Sample trips:

$800 for five days kayak, Marine Mammal Discovery.
$1,300 for seven days, Wilderness Lodge Kayak Camp.
$1,450 for ten days river rafting on the Yukon.

"Thanks for one of the best experiences of my life," wrote a woman from California. "All aspects of the Alaska trip were outstanding, exceeding my expectations entirely."

ALL-OUTDOORS WHITEWATER TRIPS

Address:	**2151 San Miguel Drive** **Walnut Creek CA 94596**
Phone:	**(415)932-8993**
Contact:	**Claudette Van Gordon**

"Our trips are not necessarily educational in nature, but people do learn to have a good time on a rafting trip," admits Ms. Gordon.

The educational side of the company's work is the Raft Guide School which trains people who want to work as guides rafting down the rivers of the West. The week-long course explains the characteristics of rivers, the differences between oar and paddle rafting, the use of the equipment, raft repair, boat rigging, river safety, and rescue procedures as well as food selection and preparation. Many of the guides leading raft trips for other companies have taken the training course.

All-Outdoors Whitewater Trips was started by the Armstrong family in 1979. Trips are offered on California's American, Merced, and Tuolomne rivers as well as trips into the Grand Canyon, to Costa Rica and to Oregon. Ecological conservation is always emphasized.

Price includes:

Accommodations, meals, lifejackets, helmets, equipment and training.

Sample trips:

$56 for half-day on American River, South Fork.
$369 for three days on Tuolumne river.
$495 for week at Guide School.
$1,613 for 13 days on Colorado through Grand Canyon.

"The guides who took our attorneys down the river were cheerful, often patient beyond the call of duty, and, of course, very professional—the event was a tremendous success," wrote a San Francisco woman after a trip down the South Fork of the American River.

AMERICAN INSTITUTE FOR FOREIGN STUDY

Address: **102 Greenwich Avenue**
Greenwich CT 06830
Phone: **(203)869-9090/(800)727-2437**
Fax: **(203)869-9615**
Contact: **Jennifer W. Fountain**

Sir Cyril H. Taylor, chairman of AIFS, considers study abroad an "international internship (which) provides valuable insight into how other peoples work and live."

AIFS is a nationwide organization that provides comprehensive overseas study and travel programs at prices the average student can afford. More than 350,000 students, teachers and interested adults have enrolled in AIFS programs in Europe, Africa, Australia, and Asia since 1964.

Membership in the Institute is open to anyone interested in study abroad.

On request, you'll receive their free 270-page College Catalog, illustrated with photos and maps explaining:

- how to apply;
- the academic requirements;
- courses for the academic year abroad;
- summer programs;
- what the campus is like;
- prices, travel details, credits.

The choices include three to 12-week summer courses, semesters of several months or an Academic Year Abroad in Australia, Britain, China, France, Italy, the Soviet Union, Spain, and other countries. In Australia, for example, university courses include seminars on Australian literature, movies, and the lives of aborigines among others. In China, students attend Peking University classes on Chinese language and literature; in Russia, students attend the Leningrad Polytechnic Institute to study language, literature, history, and political science.

AIFS has offices in Greenwich, Connecticut and San Francisco, California, and a staff of over 100 as well as part-time administrators, college admission counselors, and campus representatives.

Price includes:

Accommodations, some meals, tuition. Airfare is sometimes included.

Sample trips:

$3,949 for summer at University of New South Wales, Australia, includes airfare from Los Angeles.
$6,695 fall semester at University of Paris, France.
$12,750 academic year at Richmond College, England.

AMERICAN JEWISH CONGRESS

Address: International Travel Program
15 East 84 Street
New York NY 10028
Phone: (212)879-4588
Fax: (212)249-3672
Contact: Nancy R. Shapiro

The AJC is a community service organization committed to the eradication of all forms of prejudice, bigotry, inequality, and anti-Semitism. Membership is open to Jewish Americans over the age of 18.

The AJC/International Travel Program offers a variety of trips to places of Jewish interest, with the addition of visits to major sites and cultural attractions of each country. Whenever pre-set menus are ordered, efforts are made to avoid pork or shellfish. Saturday, the Jewish Sabbath, and other Jewish holidays are observed as days of leisure. And most of the people on the trips are Jewish.

A 16-day Mediterranean cruise visits Spain, France, Monaco, Italy, Greece, and Yugoslavia. On the tour of Kenya, participants enjoy dinner with members of the Nairobi Jewish community.

Several trips to Israel are offered, including a six-day tour of the country followed by a cruise from Haifa through the Mediterranean and across the Atlantic to Miami. Other excursions to Israel spend one to three weeks touring, and fly back. There are also special tours for families, and some trips offer special hotels for single people who are either over 30 or over 50.

In addition, AJC trips go to Egypt, Europe, Costa Rica, India, Russia, Eastern Europe, and the Orient.

Price includes:

Airfare, accommodations in hotels, all meals, tour manager, excursions, flight bag, journal, guides, transfers, taxes.

Sample trips:

$2,000 for 11 days in Israel.
$2,700 for 12 days in Eastern Europe.
$3,000 for 15 days in India.

AMERICAN MUSEUM OF NATURAL HISTORY

Address: **Discovery Tours**
Central Park West at 79th Street
New York NY 10024-5192
Phone: **(212)769-5700/(800)462-8687**
Contact: **Richard Houghton, Tours Associate**

One of the very first organizations to sponsor educational/adventure tours, the Museum now runs dozens of expeditions to Antarctica, Alaska, the Nile, Borneo, Europe, Russia, Africa, Nepal, and New Zealand, among others. Those who take the trips automatically become Museum members. Tours are limited to 18 participants, and a newsletter provides up-to-date information on upcoming expeditions. Accompanying the trips are teams of naturalists, anthropologists, astronomers, geologists, archaeologists, and art historians from the Museum and other research institutions.

Travelers can sail up the Amazon and Orinoco rivers of South America, explore the remote islands of Japan, tour the glaciers of the Antarctic Peninsula, snorkel among the coral reefs of Papua New Guinea, go birding and whale-watching along the Gulf of California, and sail around Britain to visit Ireland,

Scotland, and the Shetland Islands. Or they can choose a safari to Rwanda and Kenya to see mountain gorillas; go to North India to spot rhino, monkeys, tigers and leopards; travel to China; or trek through the volcanic South Island of New Zealand.

Price includes:

Accommodations, meals, transportation, excursions, guides, admission fees.

Sample trips:

$4,627 for three weeks in North India and Nepal.
$5,548 for two weeks on Rwanda and Kenya Safari.
$7,120 for 23 days in Papua New Guinea.

AMERICAN WILDERNESS EXPERIENCE

Address: **PO Box 1486**
Boulder CO 80306
Phone: **(303)494-2992/(800)444-0099**
Fax: **(303)494-2996**
Contact: **Dave Wiggins, President**

Established in 1971, AWE is recognized as America's oldest and largest domestic adventure travel company. It's a clearing-house and central reservation office for over 75 leading outfitters and ranches in the United States and also arranges trips for specific groups. Among those who have traveled with AWE are the Cincinnati Nature Center, the Denver Museum of Natural History, the Center for Anthropological Studies in Albuquerque, and the Colorado Mountain Club.

The catalog lists descriptions of horsepacking, white-water rafting, backpacking, llama trekking, fishing, canoeing, sea kayaking, snowmobiling, mountain biking, climbing, mountaineering, cross-country skiing, sailing, and natural history safaris offered by dozens of companies.

One of the AWE's most popular trips is a 14 day visit to the real Hawaii—you laze on sun-filled beaches, hike tree-shaded jungle trails, snorkel and swim in warm, glass-clear waters, trek over the moon-scape rocks of still-smoking Kilauea Volcano, and feast at an authentic 'luau' with flowery leis and hula dancing.

Winter programs include a sea kayaking trip in Baja California, an exploration of the Copper Canyon in Mexico, a snowmobile visit to Yellowstone National Park, and a horsepacking trip through Superstition Wilderness in Arizona.

Summer programs run the gamut from staying on ranches in Montana, Idaho, Wyoming, Arizona or Colorado to hiking trips in the Grand Canyon, plus fishing expeditions for salmon in Alaska, river rafting down Snake River in Idaho, and mountain biking in the West Virginia mountains.

AWE welcomes beginners: "The majority of our guests are first timers themselves. Our seasoned guides and wranglers will offer as much instruction and guidance as needed."

Price includes:

Accommodations, all meals, equipment and guides.

Sample trips:

$550 for five day llama trek in San Juan Mountains, Colorado.
$875 for three days snow-mobiling in Yellowstone National Park.
$950 for 11 days in Copper Canyon, Mexico.
$1,495 for 14 days in Hawaii.

AMERICAN YOUTH HOSTELS

Address: **World Adventure Trip Program**
PO Box 37613
Washington DC 20013-7613
Phone: **(202)783-6161**
Contact: **Kathy Laurin, Director**

For $25 a year, you can join the AYH no matter what your age; the word "youth" refers to your spirit. AYH members can stay at more than 200 hostels in the United States, or any of the 5000 hostels worldwide, through the International Youth Hostel Federation. A hostel is an inexpensive, dormitory-style lodging with communal kitchen and common rooms where you can meet other travelers and share your experiences.

AYH was founded in 1934; there are now over 100,000 AYH members and 39 local councils throughout the country. Every summer, AYH runs dozens of energetic bike, hike, camping and backpacking trips, and van excursions through its World Adventure Trip Program. Trip leaders are trained to share their love of travel and the outdoors. New Interpretive Trips offer in-depth explorations where travelers meet local historians, naturalists, and craftspeople.

AYH trips are divided into five categories: Adult (18 and older), 50+ (50 and older), Open (mixed ages), Youth (14 to 18) and Special Youth (12 to 13). Most trips last from one to four weeks. A few cycling and motor trips spend up to six weeks touring England, France, Netherlands, Austria, West Germany and Switzerland.

Other AYH trips include hiking in western national parks, cycling the California coast, cycling around Cape Cod, hiking the Blue Mountains in Jamaica, and exploring Mexico's Yucatan Peninsula.

Price includes:

Accommodations (in AYH hostels or low-cost lodging), meals prepared by group, transportation, trip leader. On international trips, airfare is included.

Sample trips:

$300 for nine days cycliing in New York Finger Lakes region.
$495 for nine days sailing the Florida Keys.
$700 for 22 days cycling the California coast.
$3,000 for 38 days cycling through Europe.

ANNAPOLIS SAILING SCHOOL

Address: **PO Box 3334**
601 Sixth Street
Annapolis MD 21403
Phone: **(301)267-7205/(800)638-9192**
Contact: **Peggy Murphy, Promotions Mgr.**

The oldest of the sailing schools in the United States, this company began in 1959 when there were no organized sailing schools. Now it's the largest in the country; more than 125,000 students have learned to sail there.

"We developed a simple effective way to teach beginners to sail, and refined the techniques over the years,"explains founder Jerry Wood. "We can teach you to sail through a progression of courses designed to challenge but not overwhelm your developing abilities. We have over 120 boats, a huge staff of instructors, office support staff, and marina personnel to maintain our boats."

The "Annapolis Way" of sailing instruction combines teaching by highly trained instructors with supervised hands-on practice aboard fiberglass sloops. There are no more than four students on each boat. Classes are given at several locations: Annapolis, Maryland; St. Petersburg, Florida; Marathon, Florida Keys and St. Croix, U.S. Virgin Islands. There are beginners' courses which run from two to five days; family vacation packages;

advanced courses including bareboat certification; correspondence courses in piloting and coastal navigation; and vacation packages that combine courses with hotel stays.

Price includes:

Accommodations, meals, tuition. Prices vary depending on season, cabin, and number of people on trip. Discounts for graduates of the school.

Sample trips:

$185 for weekend course, Annapolis.
$895. for winter five-day cruise, St. Croix.
$1,150 for eight-day cruise to the Dry Tortugas.

A Chicago man noted: "Classes on land and in the boats were happy, informal, fun, safe, and full of sound ideas, and we can think of no better way to spend a vacation, learning a new skill and having a pleasant time afloat."

APPALACHIAN MOUNTAIN CLUB

Address: **2 Joy Street**
Boston MA 02108.
Phone: **(617)523-0636**
Fax: **(617)523-0722**
Contact: **Director**

The Appalachian Mountain Club was created in 1876 by a group of Harvard and MIT professors who wanted to enjoy the outdoors and preserve it through geological studies, conservation projects, and land management. Today, the AMC has over 30,000 members, who are hikers, campers, bikers, rowers, conservationists, artists, and photographers with a shared concern for the outdoors.

The AMC organizes day hikes and backpacking, camping, canoeing and climbing trips for its members and the public. Many programs are held year-round at the AMC headquarters at Pinkham Notch Camp, New Hampshire, and you can call (603)466-2721 for details. This comfortable facility set in the heart of the White Mountains offers room and board for about 100 people, excellent family-style meals in a sunny dining room, and a range of activities.

In the winter, there are classes on cross-country skiing, ski touring, winter camping, and winter mountain safety. In the summer, there are dozens of excursions into the White Mountains, including week-long hut-to-hut hikes with overnights at the AMC huts spaced a day's hike apart. You can also attend classes on camping and backpacking, and lectures on such topics as Yellowstone Park fires, backcountry medicine, wolves, and bicycle touring.

Price includes:

Accommodations, meals, instruction.

Sample trips:

$90 for weekend of guided snowshoeing.
$200 for five days, Women in the Wilderness.
$265 for four days, Geology of the Presidential Range.

APPALACHIAN STATE UNIVERSITY

Address: Summer Studies Abroad
Boone NC 28608
Phone: (704)262-2810
Fax: (704)262-4037
Contact: Dr. Larry Horine

Every summer, Appalachian State University organizes programs abroad in English for both students for credit and adult learners who participate as auditors.

The courses in Britain include studying British traditional and folk music and their cultural and historical contexts, as well as accounting and international business.

In Barbados, the program involves the study of ethnographic techniques. In France, there's a business course explaining international business methods. In Germany, language classes in German at various levels are offered. In Honduras, the program involves students in Honduran social life, and they work on rural cooperative projects.

In Lugano, Switzerland, the program introduces students to the culture and experiences of life of southern Europe.

Price includes:

Airfare, accommodations, meals, tuition.

Sample trips:

$1,611 for four weeks in Barbados, living with families.
$2,766 for three weeks in England.
$2,825 for four weeks in Lugano, Switzerland.

ARCTIC TREKS

Address: **Box 73452**
Fairbanks AK 99707
Phone: **(907)455-6502**
Contact: **Carol Kasza**

As late as the 1930s, the area now known as Arctic National Park was left as blank space on maps. Today, the region epitomizes the true undeveloped wilderness; there are no roads, no trails, no campgrounds—only endless miles of wild mountains and rivers. It is part of Alaska's Brooks Range, some 600 miles long by 200 miles wide.

Arctic Treks is a family-run operation that can show you the unspoiled beauty of the Arctic Wilderness. The leaders are experienced in wilderness travel. Carol Kasza served as president of Alaska Wilderness Guides Association for four years and is a former instructor for Colorado Outward Bound School. Both she and her partner are trained in emergency medical care. Their carefully selected guides have a deep respect and admiration for the land and the people of the Arctic. Their summer trips reveal an Arctic region with no darkness, wild flowers in bloom on the tundra, migrating birds nesting, moose browsing in the willows, and caribou and Dall sheep grazing on the slopes.

You can take a backpacking and rafting expedition into the Brooks Range, just south of Mt. Doonerak, and a float down the north fork of the Koyukuk river. Or there's river rafting on the headwaters of the Noatak, the largest untouched river basin in the United States, or down the Hulahula, named by homesick Hawaiians shanghaied to work on whaling ships at the turn of the century.

A base-camp trip offers day hiking along spectacular ridges with 100-mile views in every direction and fishing for arctic char, trout, and grayling in Peters and Schrader Lakes.

"We see our role as that of the friend you've found who has a wealth of contact, knowledge, and information about this wild land—and whose attention to detail is impeccable," the leaders explain. "We feel the Brooks Range is unequaled, and we never tire of sharing it with others."

Price includes:

Airfare from Fairbanks, camping gear, all meals, rafts, equipment, guides. Tents and boots available for rent.

Sample trips:

$1,850 for 15 days backpack/rafting, Gates of Arctic.
$2,075 for seven days base camp/hiking, High Arctic.
$3,300 for 19 days, backpack/river rafting, High Arctic.

ARIZONA RAFT ADVENTURE

Address: **4050 East Huntington Drive**
Flagstaff AZ 86001
Phone: **(602)526-8200**
Fax: **(602)526-8246**
Contact: **Cathy Fenton**

This experienced company is involved in RAFT, Russians and Americans For Teamwork, a project created to establish rafting exchanges between the United States and the Soviet Union.

The company also offers rafting trips through the Grand Canyon, in Idaho, in Costa Rica, and along Mexico's Baja California. The Grand Canyon trips include eight days by motor raft, 13 days by oar and paddle rafts, and 14 days on all-paddle rafts. Other programs include a Hikers Special with many side hikes away from the river and the Gourmet Canyon Trip with a professional chef to cook along the way. They can arrange land tours of the Southwest to Bryce, Zion, and the Grand Canyon North rim as well.

In Costa Rica, there's a one-day run on the Rio Corobici, an exploration of the Carara Biological Reserve, and a ride on the Rio Pacuare with 100-foot waterfalls. And in Idaho, there are rides down the Main Salmon and Middle Fork of the Salmon River.

Price includes:

Accommodations, all meals, rafts, guides, hikes, excursions, transportation and lodging.

Sample trips:

$495 for four-day tour of Zion, Bryce, Grand Canyon.
$875 for nine days in Costa Rica.
$1,700 for 14 days through the Grand Canyon.

ARKANSAS ARTS CENTER

Address: **MacArthur Park**
10th & Commerce
PO Box 2137
Little Rock AR 72203
Phone: **(501)372-4000**
Contact: **David Nilles, Coordinator**

The Arkansas Arts Center is a nonprofit educational and cultural institution for the visual and performing arts, presenting art and crafts exhibitions in its galleries and performances in its theatre.

The Center's Decorative Arts Museum organizes Traveling Seminars every year that go to the Hudson River Valley in New York, to Egypt and its historic pyramids, and in France to the Upper Loire, Provence, and Paris.

Price includes:

Airfare, accommodations, meals, transportation, guide, entrance fees, pre-tour seminars.

Sample trip:

$3,086 for 14 days in Paris.

ARROWMONT SCHOOL OF ARTS AND CRAFTS

Address: **PO Box 567**
556 Parkway
Gatlinburg TN 37738
Phone: **(615)436-5860**
Contact: **Sandra Blain, Director**

In 1912, a group of women established a settlement school for young children in Gatlinburg, Tennessee, to commemorate the founders of Pi Beta Phi. The grateful children brought their teachers presents of handmade woven baskets and wooden carvings made by their parents. The beauty of the gifts so impressed the teachers that they established the Arrowcraft Shop in 1926 to sell local crafts. Today, the shop attracts thousands of tourists every year.

The Arrowmont School has become a nationally recognized visual arts center which attracts over 1200 students every year. The curriculum includes landscape painting, drawing, basket weaving, wood turning, coopering (making wooden buckets and tubs), quilting, weaving, paper-making, photography, stained glass, silk-screening, fabric painting, stitchery, jewelry, enameling, and blacksmithing, among others. A series of Elderhostel sessions, national and regional conferences, and classes for community residents are also held.

Situated on 70 acres of wooded hillside near the Great Smoky Mountains National Park, the facility provides large well-equipped studios; a book and supply store with tools and materials for the courses; a resource center; an auditorium; and a gallery. Students live in simple, furnished dormitory rooms in cottage-type buildings. Home-cooked meals are served in the communal dining room.

Price includes:

Accommodations (see below), all meals, tuition, facilities, activities; $50 processing fee with application.

Sample course:

$150 a week for tuition plus lab fees for materials.
$120 a week in large dorm room, $140 in a room for three, $170 in a double, or $205 in a single.

Art teacher Karen Edenfield of Palm Harbor, Florida, commented: "Arrowmont has all the answers. It offers traditional crafts but also is on top of what is contemporary. It is an oasis of fine crafts and good design."

ART INSTITUTE OF CHICAGO

Address: **Membership Programs Division**
Adams & Michigan Avenue
Chicago IL 60603
Phone: **(312)443-3616**
Fax: **(312)443-0849**
Contact: **Edith B. Gaines**

Members of the Art Institute of Chicago can join year-round travel programs to Italy, Ireland, Peru, Morocco, and Japan among several art-related tours.

"These unique programs are designed for group visits to both well-known and out-of-the-way places, featuring spectacular art, architecture, and archaeological sites," notes a staff member. "An important dimension of these trips is the enjoyment derived from sharing rewarding discoveries with fellow members and friends."

The tour of Italy focuses on the Greek, Roman, Byzantine, Moslem and Norman influences on the region with visits to Pompeii and Herculaneum. In Japan, a cruise takes the group to sacred shrines, the historic cities of Kanazawa and Kyota, and along the country's magnificent coastline. And in Turkey travelers visit the Aegean seacoast and Aphrodisias, Didyma with its Temple of Apollo, the ancient city of Ephesus, and museums in Ankara and Istanbul.

Price includes:

Airfare, accommodations, most meals, transportation, tours, guides, excursions; add $250 donation to Institute.

Sample trips:

$2,985 for two weeks in Peru.
$3,2350 for two weeks in Morocco.

ARTS ABROAD

Address: School of Visual Arts
209 East 23 Street
New York NY 10010
Phone: (212)679-7350
Fax: (212)725-3587
Contact: Anthony P. Rhodes, Director, International Studies

Imagine the soft, misty evening light of an English summer's day. Or the vivid colors and ancient buildings of China. Think of a narrow Italian street hung with washing and bright geraniums in window boxes. Dream of a stroll along the wide avenues of Barcelona. Or picture the dazzling brightness of Greece, with sunlight reflecting on white-painted houses.

If you have some artistic qualifications and experience, and long to paint abroad this summer, you can sign up for one of the courses offered by New York's School of Visual Arts program, Arts Abroad, developed by the Office of International Studies.

"We choose cities and towns of extraordinary beauty so the daily learning environment is aesthetic as well as professional," noted Anthony Rhodes, the director. "It's the creative person's vacation, creating art, and sharing it with people who understand your intent."

In Urbino, Italy, and in Barcelona, Spain, there are painting sessions for advanced students. There are courses on design and illustration in London and in Paris. And there are photography workshops in Portugal and China.

All programs include daily instruction, travel and sightseeing. The faculty are members of the international art and design community of the host country. Accommodations range from small hotels to conference centers or university residence halls, which usually provide breakfast, and students have access to the cafeteria for other meals.

Price includes:
Airfare, accommodations, transportation, tuition.

Sample trips:
$1,700 for 2 weeks in China, includes meals.
$2,700 for 3 weeks in Spain.
$2,950 for 4 weeks in Italy.

AUGUSTA HERITAGE CENTER

Address: **Davis & Elkins College**
100 Sycamore Street
Elkins WV 26241-3996
Phone: **(304)636-1903**
Contact: **Doug Hill, Publicity Coordinator**

Ever dream of playing blues guitar, crafting a quilt, or dancing Cajun style? Here's the place to learn, as well as to find out how to carve animals and birds with a knife, weave bobbin lace, or build a log house.

The Augusta program started in 1973 as a means of passing on the crafts, music, dances, and folklore traditions of Appalachia. Its name comes from the colonial-era term for the West Virginia region. Today, the Center serves as a focal point for a variety of projects -a state-wide Folk Arts Apprenticeship Program, the Augusta Heritage Records label, Elderhostel sessions, and over 100 hands-on arts classes.

The summer Augusta Heritage Arts Workshops annually attract more than 1,500 people from across the country and around the world. Special "Theme Week" music classes highlight blues, Irish, Cajun, swing, step dance, and vocal music traditions. Week-long workshops range from stained glass and stonemasonry to folk arts for children. Augusta's Spring Dulcimer Week features intensive classes in both mountain and hammered dulcimer playing, while the October Old-Time Week focuses on the Appalachian sound.

In the evenings, there are concerts, jam sessions with visiting musicians, old-time square dances and craft demonstrations. The Augusta Festival in August includes a juried crafts fair, children's activities, and a public dance under the tall oak trees of Elkins City Park.

Classes take place on the hilly, 170-acre campus of Davis and Elkins College, about five hours drive west of Washington DC. The small private liberal arts college is affiliated with the Presbyterian Church USA. Students can live on campus and take their meals in the college dining hall or stay in local motel,bed-and-breakfast or camping facilities.

Price includes:

Accommodations, all meals. Tuition separate.

Sample courses:

$145 a week for on-campus semiprivate room.
$185 to $225 a week for tuition.

BACKROADS BICYCLE TOURING

Address: **1516 5th Street, Suite Q408**
Berkeley CA 94710-1713
Phone: **(415)527-1555/(800)533-2573**
Fax: **(415) 527-1444**
Contact: **Elizabeth Gignilliat**

Established in 1978, Backroads Bicycle Touring learned how to create successful trips by perfecting every detail. Founder-director Tom Hale notes: "I personally research every new trip and new inn. I am out on more trips than ever before, spending more time with guests, assisting our leaders, and making sure that every trip we run is topnotch."

The 64-page full color catalog lists scores of different trips which last from two to 17 days. You can choose to bike in California, Alaska, Colorado, Idaho, New Mexico, Hawaii, Vermont, or Virginia in the United States, as well as in France, Ireland, Australia, Baja, Bali, China, or New Zealand.

Interesting stops along the way include a wine tasting in a Napa vineyard, exploring Santa Fe's museums and art galleries, an excursion on the narrow-gauge railroad in the Colorado Rockies, deep-sea fishing off the Kona coast of Hawaii, and a seaplane over the glaciers in New Zealand. Some tours include camping, some hotels, some overnight stays at charming inns.

Participants need ride only as far as they want and can hop into the support van when tired. Trips are rated for Beginners, Energetic Beginners, Intermediates, or Advanced with a realistic description of the terrain. Bikers choose a route and ride carrying only personal gear; everything else goes in the vans.

Special trips for singles and for families are available, and there are Prime Time Tours for older bikers. Photography workshops-on-wheels led by experienced photographers are offered in Maine, in California wine country, and in the canyons of Utah and Colorado. Some trips are designed for less energetic riders; the week-long rides in the Canadian Rockies to Point Reyes follow a very relaxed schedule. Others are more demanding; on the California Coast Inn Tour, bikers cover 50, 60, or 75 miles on some days.

Price includes:

Accommodations, all meals, safety helmet, support van, tour guides. Airfare not included. Lightweight 21-speed bikes can be rented from the company.

Sample trips:

$888 for five days in North Carolina's Outer Banks.
$926 for five days in Louisiana's Cajun Country.
$1,898 for eight days in Italy's wine district of Tuscany.

BAJA EXPEDITIONS INC.

Address: **2625 Garnet Avenue**
San Diego CA 92109
Phone: **(619)581-3311/(800)843-6967**
Fax: **(619) 581-6542**
Contact: **Director**

"The forgotten peninsula" is Baja California's nickname. It's a stark, rocky region surrounded by rippling blue seas, with abundant animal and bird life. And hundreds of whales migrate to its warm bay waters every winter. Baja Expeditions has explored the peninsula since its first trip in 1974.

The best time of year to watch migrating whales is January to April, when huge gray whales and sometimes black and white Orcas gather in the warm waters of the Sea of Cortez or Magdalena Bay.

Whale-watchers travel in the comfort of the 20-passenger vessels *Don Jose* or *Baja Explorador*. Or they can choose to paddle in kayaks and rock in the waves, camping on deserted beaches at night. But there's plenty of time to snorkel with playful sea lions, scuba dive to spot colorful fish and hike inland to discover birds nesting among craggy rocks. There are also mountain bike-riding trips along the dirt roads that wind from the Sierra to the sea.

Programs run year-round. Most popular are the week-long sea kayaking trips and the scuba-diving trips.

Photo workshops are offered as part of the Magdalena Bay whalewatching trips, when participants paddle skiffs to get close to the whales, attend evening lectures, and have film processing facilities available on board.

Baja Expeditions also offers expeditions to Costa Rica to kayak along its Pacific coast beaches and fresh-water rivers.

Price includes:

Accommodations, transportation, all meals, fishing permits, and most related trip equipment. The company can make air travel arrangements.

Sample trips:

$725 for eight days mountain biking, Baja.
$799 for nine days sea kayaking, Magdalena Bay.
$1245 for one week scuba diving, Sea of Cortez.

One woman from Oakland, California enthused after her week's kayaking: "The trip was wonderful! I thought that it would be fun but I had no idea how beautiful everything would be and what an exceptional time I would have."

BIGHORN EXPEDITIONS

Address: **PO Box 365**
Bellvue CO 80512
Phone: **(303)221-8110**
Contact: **Joan Bacon**

"Why let the guides have all the fun?" asks this experienced rafting company. Try rafting down some of the wild rivers of the American West in your own inflatable raft. You'll get some instruction before you set off, and you should be in good physical shape. Or you can sit back while their boatmen paddle.

Bighorn Expeditions offers trips down the Dolores River in south-western Colorado, through Gray and Desolation Canyons on the Green River in Utah, and along the Rio Grande River in west Texas. There are about 12 people in each group.

Price includes:

Accommodations, meals, equipment, sleeping units, tents, tuition.

Sample trips:

$595 for five days on rivers in Utah and Colorado.
$875 for eight days on rivers in Texas and Utah.

BROOKFIELD CRAFT CENTER

Address: **PO Box 122**
Route 25
Brookfield CT 06804
Phone: **(203)773-4525**
Contact: **John Russell, Executive Director**

Founded in 1954, the Brookfield Craft Center offers many unusual arts and crafts workshops year-round on its two campuses in western Connecticut. Students come from across the Northeast and mid-Atlantic states. Center membership is $25 a year, and members pay reduced fees for classes.

Evening, day, and weekend classes include metalsmithing, glassblowing, photography, woodworking, weaving, basket-making, bookbinding, ceramics, quilting, knitting, furniture construction, arts marketing, papermaking, and many other topics.

The weekend workshops have no more than 12 participants in a class. Students can work at their own pace.

"Taking one of our short weekend courses as a couple or as an individual can be a very special getaway weekend that will provide valuable educational information for continued work at home," notes Executive Director John Russell.

Price includes:

Tuition only. Add costs for lab fees and materials. Half-tuition scholarships are available. The registrar has a list of local inns and motels and there are several bed-and-breakfast places.

Sample Courses:

$85 for one day workshop on Ukrainian egg painting.
$140 for four evening classes on Amish quilts.
$140 for weekend workshop on bookbinding.

CAMP DENALI/NORTH FACE LODGE

Address: Summer: PO Box 67
Denali National Park AK 99755
Winter:Box 216 Cornish NH 03746
Phone: Summer (907)683-2290
Winter (603)675-2248
Contact: Linda Levernoch, Reservations

Set in the heart of Alaska's 5.7 million acre Denali National Park, Camp Denali is considered by many to be one of Alaska's best kept secrets. Described by guests as a place of rustic elegance, it features 18 cabins, and a centrally located dining room, lodge living room and shower facilities.

"If you want a wilderness experience away from the hectic, mechanized tempo of modern living, you'll not be disappointed," the owners promise. "Camp Denali is not for everyone. Buildings are scattered along a ridge and around a tundra pond with more concern for privacy and a view of Mt. McKinley than for convenience. You must be able to walk over uneven ground from your cabin to the lodge."

Located a mile from Camp Denali, North Face Lodge offers modern accommodations with the atmosphere of a small country inn for up to 35 people. The Lodge offers minimum stays of two or three nights while Camp Denali has three, four or five night minimum stays. Both places have spectacular views of the Alaskan Range, including Mt. McKinley, and offer opportunities for hiking, canoeing, gold panning, biking and fishing. Arrangements can be made for flight-seeing around Mt. McKinley with Lowell Thomas, Jr. and other local bush pilots, at additional cost.

Guests are met at the Park entrance and taken on an 89-mile tour with a driver/naturalist into the heart of Denali National Park, where they may see grizzly bears, Dall sheep, caribou and moose and will learn about the region's plants, geology and history.

During the summer, resident naturalists are joined by guest experts in wildflowers, nesting birds, nature photography, and the Aurora Borealis who lead seminars in the Park.

Price includes:

Accommodations, meals, transportation, activities, programs.

Sample trips:

$450 per adult for two nights/three days.
$675 per adult, three nights/four days.
$1,418 per adult for seven nights/eight days.

CANYONLANDS FIELD INSTITUTE

Address: **PO Box 68**
Moab UT 84532
Phone: **(801)259-7750**
Contact: **Karla Vander Zanden, Director of Programs**

The starkly dramatic region of the Canyonlands lies in the heart of the Colorado Plateau of southeastern Utah, close to Arches National Park and Canyonland National Park and near the canyons of the Colorado and Green Rivers.

The Canyonlands Field Institute was created in 1984 "to promote understanding and appreciation of the natural and cultural heritage of the Colorado Plateau region through seminars for adults and students." It began in association with Bates Wilson of Professor Valley Ranch near Moab, Utah, who was instrumental in gaining National Park status for Canyonlands and was its first superintendent.

CFI field-oriented seminars last from a day to a week and are led by trained naturalist-guides. Topics covered include desert weather, the lizards of Arches National Park, dinosaur tracking and literary landscapes of Canyonlands among others. Other seminars take overnight backpacking trips to explore canyons off the beaten track and writers' and photographers' workshops.

CFI also organizes a dozen week-long Elderhostel seminars each year, a summer day camp for children, and naturalist- guided walks in the National Parks.

Price includes:

All instruction and materials.

Sample trips:

$35 for one day seminar on "Salt-squeeze Geology."
$190 for four day backpack to Canyonlands Park; includes meals.
$525 for three day van tour of Navajo trading posts; includes motel and meals.

CARETTA RESEARCH PROJECT

Address: **4405 Paulsen Street**
Savannah GA 31405
Phone: **(912)355-6705**
Contact: **Win Seyle, Director**

The Caretta Research Project is a hands-on research and conservation program aimed at saving the loggerhead sea turtle, known scientifically by its Latin name of *Caretta caretta.*

The project began in 1973 and operates under a cooperative agreement with the U.S. Fish and Wildlife Service, Department of the Interior.

Its goals are:

1) to learn more about population levels, trends and habits of the loggerhead turtle;

2) to enhance survival of eggs and hatchlings on a nesting beach;

3) to get members of the public involved in the work.

Volunteers come to the island for one-week sessions from mid-May through early October every year. Working in small groups with a leader, they move and protect some nests, monitor the nests after the eggs are laid, and later escort the newly-hatched turtles to the surf. During the day, they check and maintain numbered beach markers, inspect nests for predators or storm damage, dig up and record contents of hatched nests, and survey the beaches for dead turtles.

Director Win Seyle stressed, "This is a volunteer work project, *not* a vacation opportunity," and explained: "During egg-laying (mid-May to mid-August) you will spend most of each night patrolling Wassaw Island's six miles of beaches, searching for the huge female loggerheads as they crawl out of the surf to nest. You and your research team will tag each turtle, take measurements of the turtle and its path to the nest, and record other important information."

Participants should be able to walk a few miles along a beach at night using natural light, not a flashlight. Past experience shows that cheerful, upbeat, adaptable people cope best with the crowded conditions (participants live in two small cabins), and with insects, rainstorms, heat, and humidity. So far, some 1,200 volunteers have taken part in the project.

Price includes:

Accommodations, all meals, training, transportation, van from the Savannah Science Museum to island and back.

Sample trips:

$375 for one week, May to August.
$300 for one week, September to October.

CASA XELAJU DE ESPANOL

Address: **PO Box 11264**
Milwaukee WI 53211
Phone: **(414)372-5570**
Fax: **(414)372-5570**
Contact: **Julio E. Batres**

The Casa Xelaju is a year-round Spanish-language school in Guatemala for students of all ages which also offers programs on the country's social, cultural, and political background. Situated in Quetzaltenanago, the Spanish language classes run for five hours daily. Courses start every Monday, with a one-to-one ratio of teachers to students, at all levels of Spanish.

Special classes teach Mam and Quiche, indigenous languages of different regions of Guatemala. There are courses on backstrap weaving and Guatemalan cooking and concerts with music and dancing featuring a marimba band. Field trips take students to Guatemala City, to explore the rain forest, to climb Volcano Santa Maria, to San Martin Chile Verde for Ascension Day in the Indian community, and to the state of Totonicapan to celebrate the Mayan New Year.

Price includes:

Accommodations, meals, laundry, tuition, educational materials, activities, field trips, movies, marimba band concerts.

Sample trips:

$350 for 2 weeks.
$520 for 3 weeks.
$660 for a month; reduced rates for several months.

"Casa Xelaju exudes warmth," wrote one teacher, "from the families, from the teachers, from the whole town. In this relaxed, comradely atmosphere I have soaked up Spanish and learned a lot about Guatemala."

CENTER FOR ENGLISH STUDIES

Address: International House
330 Seventh Avenue
New York NY 10001
Phone: (212)620-0760
Fax: (212)594-7415
Contact: Michael Stark, Study Abroad Coordinator

The CES School of Languages is a nationally accredited school teaching English to non-English-speaking students or to those who want to improve and perfect their English-language skills. The CES Foreign Language Division offers private instruction in several languages in New York. Its four-week summer International Teachers Training Institute qualifies teachers to teach English in IH schools in more than 20 foreign countries.

In conjunction with language schools abroad, it offers Study Abroad programs throughout the year in Europe and, new this year, a summer Arabic program in Egypt.

There are CES Spanish courses in Barcelona, Madrid, and Majorca, in Portuguese in Lisbon, and in Italian in Rome, Siena, Sicily, and on Ventotene, a island about 60 miles from Rome. French courses are offered in Antibes and Tours, and German in Switzerland and in Freiburg, Germany. All centers offer daily language classes and cultural and other excursions. Participants stay with local families, or in student residences.

Price includes:

Tuition only, though varies from school to school. Brochure prices are listed in local currencies.

Sample trips:

$500 for four weeks of German in Lugano, Switzerland, plus $141 a week for family stay.

$144 for two weeks of Italian in Ventotene, Italy, plus $720 for room, board, and boating equipment.

CENTRO DI CULTURA ITALIANA CASENTINO

Address: c/o Stephen Casale
One University Place, Apt. 17-R
New York NY 10003
Phone: (212)228-9273
Contact: Stephen Casale

In the northeastern part of Tuscany in Italy, between Florence and Arezzo, is the medieval town of Poppi. It sits atop a hill above the rolling valleys, the square tower of its dramatic castle visible for miles around. Poppi is ideally suited for those who wish to see the work of Piero della Francesca and other Renaissance artists in churches and museums nearby.

The Centro di Cultura Italiana Casentino was founded in 1980 in collaboration with the town and offers intensive Italian-language courses. Classes run for two or four weeks between June and October, with four hours of instruction every morning Monday through Friday, followed by visits to historic sights in the afternoon. Every evening except Wednesday and Saturday, students, teachers and other Italian friends dine together at the Ristorante Casentino near the castle, enjoying Tuscan cuisine with homemade pasta, fresh vegetables, and salads. Students stay with Italian families, or they can rent a furnished apartment in a historical center reserved for the school or in a country house near Poppi.

Students can also swim, ride horses, hike, or play golf, volleyball, tennis or basketball. Almost every weekend, there are village festivals, like the feast of the Porcino mushroom, when everyone celebrates with food, drink, music, and dancing in the piazza.

Price includes:

Accommodations, most meals, tuition, activities, excursions. Prices are approximate; tuition is paid in Italian currency.

Sample courses:

$750 for two weeks.
$1,390 for four weeks.

"Whoever wants to really study Italian and at the same time get to know the country and its people will find the CCIC the perfect place to do it," wrote one participant.

CENTRUM FOUNDATION

Address: **PO Box 1158**
Port Townsend WA 98368
Phone: **(206)385-3102**
Contact: **Carla Vander Ven**

Centrum is set on 330 acres of Fort Worden State Park in Washington, about 50 miles from downtown Seattle, and was established in 1973 as a nonprofit arts center. Though the ocean is too cold for swimming, there's sailing and lovely walks along the beach and around the park, with stunning views of the Olympic Mountains in the distance.

Centrum offers month-long creative residencies for artists, and performances by musicians, both jazz and classical. Every summer it presents more than 70 events, including symphony concerts and theater productions, as well as educational courses in music, jazz, theater, dance, and writing, with about six Elderhostel sessions. There's a fiddle tunes workshop, and a ten-day workshop for writers, among others, and they're always filled to capacity.

Price includes:

Tuition only. Dormitory rooms (rent linens for $9 a week) and meal service available for about $155 per week. Housing list on request.

Sample Courses:

$150 for eight-day Festival of American Fiddle tunes.
$225 for eight-day Jazz Workshop.
$270 for ten-day Writers' Conference.

Elizabeth Sandvig, an artist in residence, commented; "The jewel-like natural setting, the isolation from the hazards of urban life, and the excellent working conditions provide a unique opportunity for an artist."

CLEVELAND INSTITUTE OF ART

Address: **Foreign Study Office**
11141 East Boulevard
Cleveland OH 44106
Phone: **(216)229-0938**
Fax: **(216)229-0905**
Contact: **Jennifer L. Tucker, Foreign Study Coordinator**

The Institute offers a unique educational experience in which artists live and work in Lacoste, a tiny medieval village 25 miles north of Avignon in France's Provence region. Amid these rolling landscapes Cezanne, Van Gogh, Gauguin, Man Ray, Alexander Calder and Picasso once lived and worked. The Cleveland Institute of Art offers undergraduates, graduates and independent students a 15-week semester at Lacoste in the fall and a six-week summer session.

The art center in Lacoste was founded by American surrealist painter Bernard Pfriem in 1971. He arrived in the 1950s, bought an abandoned house for $50, added the ruined building next door and the nearby bakery, and installed the first art studio. Today, the school occupies a network of 19 buildings, and attracts between 40 and 80 students a year.

"People come here for the area, to focus and concentrate on their work and be extremely productive," says an artist from California, who came to Lacoste in 1981 and now works in the printmaking studio. "There are very few distractions, and there's a lot of time for contemplation and reflection."

A fall and spring semester in Florence is also available through Studio Arts Center International for undergraduate and independent students, plus an early summer course in Florence and a tour of Europe's museums led by an art historian.

Price includes:

Accommodations, all meals, tuition, excursions. Some scholarships available.

Sample courses:

$2,550 to $5,900, depending on length of stay.

A graduate of Smith College noted, "As an older student, I loved being with the younger students. It was very invigorating and mentally stimulating. I am now in the process of digesting all the wonderful things I saw, learned and did."

COMPTON COMMUNITY COLLEGE

Address: **Summer Study Program**
1111 East Artesia Boulevard
Compton CA 90221-5393
Phone: **(213)637-2660/Ext.314/388**
Fax: **(213)608-3721**
Contact: **Dr. Bill Hart**

Every summer since 1973, Dr. Hart has organized a study program either in Madrid, Spain or in Cuernavaca, Mexico for high-school seniors, college students and other interested adults;

the average age is usually around 31. The program is held in cooperation with the Cemanahuac Comunidad Educativa and offers Spanish-language courses and an introduction to Mexican culture. Students live with middle-class Mexican families, with all meals provided.

Language classes are limited to five students, from beginner to advanced levels based on placement tests, and are held five days a week from 9 a.m. to 1 p.m. There are conversation classes from 1 to 2 p.m. followed at 4 or 5 p.m. with classes in Mexican history, culture, politics, current events and more, some given in Spanish and some in English. Gabriela de la Paz, a popular Mexican singer-guitarist, teaches Mexican and Latin American songs.

From Cuernavaca, known as "The City of Eternal Spring," students travel to Oaxaca during the annual folk dance festival, to Merida with its ancient Mayan pyramids, and to Cancun on the shores of the Caribbean ocean.

Price includes:

Airfare, accommodations, all meals, tuition, transportation, excursions, hotels, entrance fees, guided tours. Dr. Hart notes that so few people apply for scholarships that they are almost always available to qualified applicants.

Sample trips:

$1,345 for four weeks in Cuernavaca.

CONSORTIUM FOR INTERNATIONAL EDUCATION

Address: 2061 Business Center Drive #209
Irvine CA 92713
Phone: (714)955-1700
Fax: (714)955-2945
Contact: Cathy Fagan, Associate V.P.

Acting as a travel agent, the Consortium offers programs abroad to students attending several colleges. Students choose semesters lasting several months or shorter trips of a few weeks. Institutions associated with CIE include California's Santa Monica College, Fresno City College, Orange Coast College, Pasadena City College, and Los Angeles Community College, plus Lake City College in Florida.

Consortium trips include semesters in Oxford, England, with travel to London and the Lake District. In Costa Rica, students go to the Central American Institute for International Affairs in San Jose to study Spanish and biology. There's a semester in Vienna focusing on music, and one at Negev College in Israel.

Shorter trips offer three weeks in China or Scandinavia, two and four week sessions learning Spanish in Spain, two weeks in Australia, ten days on an architectural tour of Mexico's Yucatan, a week in Singapore for the Food and Hotel Asia International Salon Culinaire, and a week's tour of English gardens.

Price includes:

Airfare from Los Angeles, accommodations, some meals, transportation, tuition, tour guides.

Sample trips:

$1,995 for four-week language program in Spain.
$2,682 for three weeks in Europe (from New York).
$3,282 for two weeks exploring Australia.
$3,790 for semester in Costa Rica.

CORNELL'S ADULT UNIVERSITY

Address: **626 Thurston Avenue**
Ithaca NY 14850
Phone: **(607)255-6260**
Fax: **(607)255-7533**
Contact: **Ralph Janis, Director**

"Our summer family program is the largest and one of the oldest programs of its type in the United States," says Ralph Janis, director of Cornell's Adult University.

Every summer since 1968, week-long seminars and workshops, led by Cornell's finest scholars and teachers, are offered on the beautiful campus in Ithaca, in the Finger Lakes district of New York State. A total of 28 courses for adults cover "Great Books: War and Peace," "Archaeology: Recovering the Past," "Pedal-Power Paleontology," and "Making It: Success in America."

Of those who attend, two-thirds are couples, and the rest single. About half of the participants bring youngsters. CAU provides a Youth Program with special classes designed for children from three to seventeen.

The excellent recreational facilities of the Cornell campus—gorges, hiking trails, lake for boating, tennis courts, golf, and more—are available to participants, and they can attend the plays, concerts, and other cultural events which take place daily on campus.

CAU also sponsors a variety of seminars and study-tours outside Ithaca, both in the United States and abroad. Programs for 1990 include a two-week study tour to Spain and North Africa, two weeks studying the art of Belgium and the Netherlands, a week in New Mexico examining culture and natural history, five-day seminars on marine biology and ecology at the Shoals Marine Laboratory in Maine, and a five-day seminar in Hollywood, California. Programs usually fill quickly, and there's always a waiting list.

Price includes:

Accommodations, all meals, academic program, facilities, events, transportation, site visits.

Sample trips:

$550 for a week at Ithaca, NY.
$625 for five days at Shoals Marine Laboratory.
$995 for a week in New Mexico.
$2,890 for two weeks in Belgium
$5,195 for two weeks in Spain and North Africa.

From those who've taken the week-long seminars, comments include: "Superb teaching and incredible group camaraderie," and "What college is supposed to be but rarely is." One woman confessed: "My children were crying when it was time to leave."

COUNCIL FOR INTERNATIONAL EDUCATION

Address: **326 South 500 East**
Salt Lake City UT 84102
Phone: **(801)355-3630**
Fax: **(801)355-7436**
Contact: **Ray Phillips**

The CIE, a not-for-profit organization coordinating academic courses in Europe, Asia, and South America, has conducted 146 programs in cities throughout the world since it began in 1969.

A university professor directs and escorts each course and acts as academic advisor. College students from the United States and other parts of the world participate in the program. In the special January sessions, designed for colleges on the "4-1-4" semester program, students can choose to sketch and draw in

Paris, study the European Economic Community, or take a seminar on London Theater for 4 weeks.

Price includes:

Airfare, tuition, accommodations (hotel or student residence), tours, excursions, some meals.

Sample trips:

$1,495 for four weeks studying French civilization.
$1,575 for four weeks in London, five days in Paris.
$1,895 for four weeks studying European Economic Community.

COUNCIL ON INTERNATIONAL EDUCATIONAL EXCHANGE

Address: **205 East 42nd Street**
New York NY 10017
Phone: **(212)661-1414**
Fax: **(212)972-3231**
Contact: **Council Travel (212)661-1450**

Established in 1947 by a group of organizations active in international education and student travel, CIEE is now a large private, not-for-profit membership organization which develops, facilitates and administers programs of international educational exchange throughout the world as well as providing counseling and information services. It also conducts research; publishes studies, brochures and books; organizes conferences; and provides assistance to educational organizations.

Council Travel is the travel division of CIEE. It is one of the largest budget travel organizations in America and has helped millions of students, teachers, and other travelers with their plans. CIEE's annual *Student Travel Catalog* provides essential information about travel abroad, work abroad, international workcamps, study courses, and volunteer programs.

There are 30 CIEE offices around the United States and offices in England, France, Germany, and Japan. Services include low-cost airfares, rail passes, tours, low-cost car rentals, accommodations, and insurance. They also issue International Student Identity Cards and International Youth Identity Cards.

CIEE is an excellent resource for budget-minded international travelers. As well as the free catalog, they offer information on airfares, hotels, tours, study programs at Eurocentres, and a newsletter, *The Budget Traveler*.

Price includes:

Accommodations, tuition, activities.

Sample trips(at Eurocentres):

$975 for four weeks studying French in Paris.
$1,500 for 12 weeks studying Spanish in Madrid.

CROW CANYON ARCHAEOLOGICAL CENTER

Address: **23390 Country Road K**
Cortez CO 81321
Phone: **(303)565-8975**
Contact: **Ian Thompson, Executive Director**

At the beginning of the 12th century, there were at least 10,000 people living on and around the Mesa Verde Plateau in Southwestern Colorado. By the end of the 13th century, there were none; a complex farming culture had vanished from a hauntingly beautiful land where it had flourished for more than a thousand years. Those ancient people, the Anasazi, left no written account of their remarkable stay. But they did leave behind deserted communities built of stone, filled with the items of daily life.

Archaeologists at Crow Canyon Archaeological Center are conducting important long-term research focused on the events leading up to the final Anaszai abandonment of the Mesa Verde region by the year 1300. They welcome interested students and adults to assist them with work at the excavation sites and in the laboratory.

Crow Canyon also offers archaeo-botanical programs, which assess the impact of prehistoric environmental change on the adaptive strategies of the Anasazi and contribute to a greater understanding of the modern environment of the Four Corners area.

"There is no need for previous experience in archaeology," explains Ian Thompson, Executive Director. "Every year, hundreds of novices, ranging from young adults to retirees, participate in our research."

The excavation and botanical programs run from mid-May to mid-October. Participants work for a week or longer. Year-round programs explore the richness of the Native American tradition and the grandeur of this remote yet magnificent landscape, where native Americans have lived for over a thousand years.

Price includes:

Accommodations, meals, tuition, equipment.

Sample trips:

$690 for one-week excavation/botanical program.
$1,095 for one-week exploration program.

CUAUHNAHUAC-MEXICO

Address: **Instituto Colectivo de lengua y cultura**
519 Park Drive
Kenilworth IL 60043
Phone: **(708)256-7570**
Contact: **Marcia Snell, U.S. Representative**

Cuauhnahuac is the original name for Cuernavaca in Mexico, where this language institute, founded in 1972, offers intensive programs in the Spanish language and Mexican culture. Credit affiliation is with Northeastern Illinois University and the University of La Verne.

Class size is limited to four students with five hours of daily classroom instruction. Every week, there are three hours of grammar, an hour of vocabulary, writing, pronunciation, reading, and idiomatic expressions, and an hour of conversation. The full course runs for 12 to 16 weeks, but students can sign up for shorter periods.

The instructors, all Mexicans, speak only Spanish during classes. Students can have private instruction on an individual basis. In the afternoons, there are minicourses on Mexican history, linguistics and literature, cooking, folk dancing and folk songs. Informal discussions in Spanish cover the politics, folklore, and customs of Mexico and Latin America. Excursions are available to places of interest nearby—the Xochicalco pyramids, the colonial town of Taxco, the Indian village of Tepotzlan—as well as to concerts, plays, films, and fiestas.

Cuauhnahuac is housed in a colonial building with classrooms, library, recreation room, lecture hall, a spacious garden, a swimming pool, and a volleyball court. An independently run restaurant provides food. Students come from all over the world and include high-school and university students, teachers, diplomats, and retirees. Most live with Mexican families recommended by the Institute.

Price includes:

Accommodations with Mexican family, all meals, tuition. Add $60 registration fee.

Sample costs:

$84 for shared room/$126 for separate room. $135 for a week's tuition.
$500 for a month's tuition.

DENVER MUSEUM OF NATURAL HISTORY

Address: **Travel Study Trips**
2001 Colorado Boulevard
Denver CO 80205
Phone: **(303)370-6303**
Fax: **(303)331-6492**
Contact: **Patricia C. Holwell, Domestic Travel Coordinator**

You can join the Denver Museum of Natural History for $30 a year, or $40 as a family, and be eligible to travel with them. The Museum organizes about 16 travel study trips a year.

The range is wide: camping, tours to Europe and Asia, river rafting, archeological expeditions, cultural visits, a serious buyer's trip of Indian arts and crafts in the American Southwest. All are accompanied by qualified study leaders.

Domestic excursions go to Manitou Grand Cavern for spelunking in Jackson Hole, bird-watching on the eastern plains for bald and golden eagles, kestrels and hawks; and a week's rafting down the Yampa River. Abroad, members go to the

Copper Canyon region of Mexico's Sierra Madres, on an archaeological tour of Guatemala led by a leading pre-Columbian scholar, and to Siam to see wild orchids growing in mist-covered mountains and exotic tribespeople in black turbans and silver jewelry.

Price includes:

Airfare, accommodations, meals, transportation, guides, entrance fees. Prices include a donation to the Museum.

Sample trips:

$495 for five days rafting down Yampa River.
$1,753 for eight days in Copper Canyon, Mexico.
$4,822 for 18 days in Thailand.
$7,500 for three weeks in Tanzania and Zimbabwe.

DILLMAN'S CREATIVE WORKSHOPS

Address: **PO Box 98**
Lac du Flambeau WI 54538
Phone: **(715)588-3143/(800)433-6772**
Contact: **Sue Robertson**

Mary and Peg Dillman started Dillman's Sand Lake Lodge in 1935, and it has become a successful family-run vacation resort. The lodge is set on a peninsula of Northern Wisconsin surrounded by acres of woodlands.

The Creative Workshops began in 1977 and every summer from May to October offer a schedule of dozens of summer classes in water colors, portrait painting, how to sell artwork, painting with pastels and acrylics, quilting, carving, and photography.

Students live in the lakeside vacation homes, inn rooms, or dorm units. The area has hiking trails, tennis courts, golf courses, horseback riding, bowling, summer theaters, and museums nearby. There is fishing and free water skiing.

Price includes:

Accommodations, all meals, facilities, tuition for one workshop. Non-participants pay $417 for six-day stay.

Sample courses:

$465 for four days, Native American Arts.
$555 for five days, Multi-Media Landscape.
$575 for five days, Watercolor & Drawing.
$620 for five days, Reviewing Basic Photography.

EARTHWATCH

Address: **PO Box 403N**
680 Mt. Auburn Street
Watertown MA 02272
Phone: **(617)926-8200**
Fax: **(617)926-8532**
Contact: **Kara Bettigole**

"Never will I look at elephants the same way. They will always remind me of their ancestral relatives, the Columbian Mammoths and their bones lying 'in situ' at the Mammoth Site."

This comment comes from an Earthwatch volunteer who worked with paleontologists in South Dakota. Earthwatch offers ordinary people the chance to be active participants in environmental research projects around the world. It is affiliated with the Center for Field Research, which receives hundreds of proposals from scientists who need help.

Earthwatch provides the volunteers. The idea is that those who work on the projects will understand the significance of research efforts to preserve our environment.

You can join Earthwatch for $25 a year. Members receive the bi-monthly magazine and choose a project that needs help. These include capturing, tranquilizing, and examining black bears in North Carolina's Pisgah Bear Sanctuary; observing the diet of captive musk oxen and caribou in Fairbanks, Alaska; and photographing whales in the Hawaiian islands. Overseas, volunteers work on developing an education program to save the cranes of Vietnam. In England, an archeological hunt looks for tools, coins, pottery, and Roman artifacts along the miles of Hadrian's wall. In Egypt, there's an excavation of the 3,300-year-old tomb of Amenhotep Huy in a desert oasis and, in Western Australia, a study of native wildlife.

Founded in 1971 as a bridge between the public and the scientific community, Earthwatch has sent 23,000 volunteers on hundreds of projects in 85 countries and 36 states. Volunteers range in age from 16 to 85. One woman has joined 25 expeditions!

Earthwatch also raises funds from corporations, foundations, and individuals to provide fellowships for teachers and students; in 1989, 167 teachers and 85 students received fellowships.

Price includes:

Accommodations, all meals, instruction. A contribution ranging from $800 to $2,000 is included. Participants pay their own travel costs.

Sample trips:

$990 for two weeks, wildlife survey, Shenandoah Valley.
$1,145 for two weeks, bear project, North Carolina.
$2,240 for two weeks saving cranes in Vietnam.

EASTERN MICHIGAN UNIVERSITY

Address: **Office of International Studies**
333 Godison
Ypsilanti MI 48197
Phone: **(313)487-2424/(800)777-3541**
Fax: **(313)487-2316**
Contact: **Joyce Combs, Asst. to Director**

Among several programs, Eastern Michigan University offers a unique six-week European Cultural History Tour. Students must enroll in at least one three-hour course for credit, choosing history, art-appreciation, or art and architecture.

The travel-packed tour includes stops in London, Paris, and Cologne; a cruise down the Rhine River; visits to East and West Berlin; and then on to Prague, Vienna, Salzburg and Munich. Students spend two days in the mountains of the Austrian Tyrol; a few days in Venice, Florence, and Rome; visit Greece, Turkey, and Israel and ride across the Sinai Desert to Egypt to explore the ancient tombs of Luxor and the city of Cairo.

Other EMU summer programs include a German-language course in two German cities with a week of travel; Spanish language study in Cuernavaca, Mexico; and a course in art history and drawing in Florence, Italy.

There's also a two-week excursion to the Galapagos Islands; a tour of Russia and Poland with visits to Leningrad, Kiev, Moscow, Warsaw and Prague; and a 16 weeks fall semester Interdisciplinary Humanities Tour of Europe, Israel, and Egypt.

Price includes:

Accommodations, transportation, tuition, field trips, excursions, tickets to events, museum entrance fees, International Student ID Card, breakfast and one other meal a day, visa fees, service charges, local taxes.

Sample trips:

$2,995 for 23 days, Russia and Poland; includes airfare.
$2,995 for 13 days, Galapagos Islands, from Florida.
$3,995 for 74 days, European Cultural History Tour.

One student who took the European Cultural Tour said: "I just graduated from the University of Michigan and I feel this trip was a perfect way to augment my education. I thoroughly explored the cities with their outstanding museums, cathedrals and palaces. I became absorbed in the countless operas, dance musicals and concerts we so often attended. Each day offered enriching activities and I am still literally astounded by how much we accomplished."

ECHO: The Wilderness Company

Address: **6259 Telegraph Avenue**
Oakland CA 94609
Phone: **(415)652-1600**
Contact: **Joe Daly**

ECHO was founded in 1971 by Joe Daly and Dick Linford and offers trips on several rivers, including the Salmon in Idaho, the American and Tuolumne in California, and the Rogue River in Oregon. Some include a special educational emphasis, such as the "White (and Red) Wine and Whitewater" excursion, on which a California winemaker brings wines to taste between the rapids. Other trips offer music along the way, provided by the Salmon River Blue Grass group with fiddle, mandolin, and banjo, and classical music with the Rogue River String Quartet.

The "Klutz Fun-Festival" introduces John Cassidy, president of Klutz Enterprises, who teaches rafters how to juggle, play Hacky-Sacky, and blow a harmonica. There's also a trip specially designed to teach kids camping and river skills.

The company joins with Backroads Bicycle touring to offer a "Pedals and Paddles" excursion with five days of cycling in Idaho's spectacular Sawtooth Mountains followed by six days of white water rafting on the Main Salmon.

Price includes:

Accommodations, all meals, transportation, guides, equipment, entertainment.

Sample trips:

$379 for three days on the Tuolumne River, California.
$549 for five days on the Rogue River, Oregon.
$1,486 for 12 days on the Salmon River, Idaho.

"ECHO trips are the best therapy for the country soul trapped in a city slicker's body" was one comment from a participant after rafting down the river.

EDINBORO AT OXFORD EXPERIENCE

Address: **Edinboro University**
102 Doucette Hall
Edinboro PA 16444
Phone: **(814)732-2884**
Fax: **(814)732-2294**
Contact: **Ted Atkinson**

American students who dream of walking along the historic streets of Oxford and studying in its ancient colleges can do so through Edinboro University's two week summer program there.

Students live and study in Exeter College, the fourth oldest college at Oxford University, dating back to 1314, and take classes in English literature, archeology, art, or education. They stay in private rooms at the college, eat dinner every evening in the baronial dining hall, and have plenty of opportunity to explore the buildings, museums, and historic sights of Oxford.

The program relates the content of the courses to the people and culture that helped to shape it. Its aim is to integrate the academic and intercultural experiences. For example, a course on English literature examines the work of Chaucer and Shakespeare and takes students to visit Canterbury and Stratford-upon-Avon.

Price includes:

Airfare from New York, accommodations, all meals, transportation, tuition, activities and excursions.

Sample trip:

$1,900 for two weeks of Edinboro at Oxford Experience.

ELDERHOSTEL

Address: **80 Boylston Street**
Suite 400
Boston MA 02116
Phone: **(617)426-7788**
Fax: **(617)426-8351**
Contact: **Information Director**

"Retirement does not represent an end, but a new beginning filled with opportunities and challenges," is the philosophy of Elderhostel. Founded in 1975 in New Hampshire by Marty Knowlton to provide educational vacations for adults over 60 who want to expand their horizons and develop new interests,

Elderhostel has grown into an international network of enthusiastic supporters.

Today, over 1,500 colleges, universities, and other institutions offers hundreds of Elderhostel courses in the United States and abroad. Almost 200,000 people took Elderhostel courses in 1989, living in dorm rooms on university and college campuses. One couple in their 70s who have attended 20 programs commented: "It's not a freebie or a cheap vacation. It's set up so that you must keep your brains expanding."

The Boston office deals with general administration, publishes three issues a year of the bulky catalog and three issues of the newsletter *Between Classes*. The educational institutions provide the course curriculum and the faculty. The most popular programs are those on modern history, creative writing, and appreciation of opera, music and paintings. Courses include "The Life and Customs of the Hopi," "Power of the Mind in Health and Illness," "A Zen Buddhist Experience," "Cross-Country Skiing," "Forensic Anthropology," and "Radio in the Golden Years."

Programs are offered in Britain, Scandinavia, Greece, and Italy as well as in Argentina, Australia, Finland, Israel, Nepal, Sweden, and Russia, among others, with Saga Holidays as overseas tour operators for Elderhostel.

Price includes:

Airfare, registration, accommodations, all meals, classes, facilities, activities.

Sample trips:

$245 for one week is average rate on all US campuses.
$2,775 for three weeks in Scandinavia.
$5,075 for four weeks in Australia and New Zealand.

One Michigan woman commented: "Elderhostel has been great for me, a woman who has spent most of her life cooking, cleaning and chauffeuring, to associate with learned professors, engineers, poets, authors, librarians, and doctors. To listen to their conversations and feel free to enter in at will is a privilege."

EUROPA-KOLLEG KASSEL

Address: c/o Kuhn-Osius
230 West 105 Street Apt. 7B
New York NY 10025
Phone: (212)865-7332
Contact: Professor Eckhard Kuhn-Osius

Europa-Kolleg is a nonprofit German-language institute founded in 1967 in the city of Kassel, between Hanover and Frankfurt. The city is famous as the place where the Brothers Grimm wrote their fairy tales. Kassel was also the city from which soldiers were sold to the British to fight in America's War of Independence. Part of the money was spent to establish parks and art collections.

Over 20,000 students from 80 different countries have taken the Europa-Kolleg language courses. Anyone over 16 is eligible to participate throughout the year. The basic intensive language course lasts 11 weeks. During the summer, there are shorter courses which can be taken successively. Language classes are held every morning, and in the afternoons students may attend seminars on literature, visit places of local interest, explore the surrounding countryside, or go to movies and theatre. Students live with German families.

Price includes:

Accommodations, all meals, tuition, extra-curricular activities.

Sample courses:

$312 for one week of instruction.
$1,250 for four weeks of language and culture course.
$3,430 for 11 weeks of language and culture course.

EXPEDITIONS INC.

Address: **625 N Beaver Street**
Flagstaff AZ 86001
Phone: **(602)779-3769/(602)774-8176**
Contact: **Dick and Susie McCallum**

Dick McCallum has traveled and explored rivers from Alaska to South America for over 30 years and says, "For me, the Grand Canyon will always be **the** special place."

He and his wife specialize in educational river-running trips through the Grand Canyon, since they were both in public education before establishing their company. They enjoy guiding as many of the river trips as possible. The company is an authorized National Park Service concessionaire.

Trips last from five to 14 days on oar-powered inflatable boats. The longer ones explore the entire Grand Canyon, from Lees Ferry to the take-out point 226 miles below at Diamond Creek. The shorter ones require hiking in or out at the South Rim on the Bright Angel or Kaibab Trail. Both include hiking along side canyons, swimming, and camping under the stars.

Price includes:

Transportation from Flagstaff and back, sleeping gear, all meals, guides, boats. Tents available for rent.

Sample trips:

$650 for five days on the river.
$1,050 for eight days on the river.
$1,680 for 14 days on the river.

One participant wrote: "I've traveled all my life, but this was definitely the best trip ever. Since I've been home, I can't stop talking about it. The experience of the Grand Canyon atmosphere put me on a natural high for months."

EXPERIMENT IN INTERNATIONAL LIVING

Address: **Summer Abroad**
PO Box 676
Brattleboro VT 05302
Phone: **(802 257-7751**
Contact: **Michael Koonce**

The essence of the Experiment's approach is that participants go to another country to live with families, speak their language, and experience their way of life. Since 1932, when Dr. Donald Watt founded the organization, thousands of young people have taken part in these exchanges. Today, the Experiment has more than 40 offices around the world, runs a School for International Training offering both undergraduate and graduate degree programs, and offers dozens of summer programs for high-school and college-age students. These include:

- Classic Homestay, where students live with a family in Denmark, France, Germany, Great Britain, Ireland, Italy, Mexico, Spain, or Switzerland for four weeks. Additions to the Homestay include a two-week language study program, or a two-week multiple country travel option.

- Homestay Adventure, a set program for four or six weeks which includes Homestay and travel, available in France, Italy, Spain, Switzerland, Australia, and Ecuador.

- Summer Study, in which students take a six-week language and culture courses combined with a Homestay for college credit. Travel may be added.

The travel itinerary varies in every country. In Australia, students visit the Outback, Kakadu National Park, and the Great Barrier Reef. In Ecuador, the group tours the Galapagos Islands and the markets and weavings of Otavalo. After the French Homestay, the group visits Amsterdam, Hamburg, Berlin, Munich, Heidelberg, and Brussels.

Price includes:

Airfare, orientation, accommodations, all meals, transportation, excursions, admission fees, insurance. There is a non-refundable $75 application fee.

Sample trips:

$1,100 for Classic Homestay in Mexico.
$4,100 for Homestay Adventure in Italy.
$4,700 for Summer Study in France.
$6,300 for Summer Study in Kenya.

EYE OF THE WHALE

Address: **PO Box 1269**
Kapa'au HI 96755
Phone: **(808)889-0227/800)657-7730**
Contact: **Mark and Beth Goodoni**

This company offers a very different view of Hawaii from the glitter and dazzle of Honolulu's skyscrapers. Eye of the Whale has designed tours to explore the unhurried, unspoiled, and less-well-known parts of these unique islands.

Beth has a master's degree in physiology and behavioral biology. She has taught field classes in marine mammal biology, and conducted research on humpback and killer whales in Alaska and bottlenose dolphins in the Gulf of Mexico. Mark Goodoni has a degree in marine resource development, and trained as an Outward Bound instructor and wilderness emergency medical technician. He is also a USCG licensed captain. They hope their tours will develop awareness, appreciation, and understanding of Hawaii's delicate ecosystem.

The Goodonis lead small groups of 10 or fewer on a five-day sailing trip off the west coast of the Big Island of Hawaii looking for spotted and spinner dolphins, and humpbacked whales, with nights spent anchored in secluded coves. They also offer a seven-day "Earth, Fire & Sea" excursion which begins at Kailua-Kona, visits the dramatic cliffs of the Waipio Valley, explores Volcanoes National Park, and includes three days of cruising aboard a sailboat.

The ten-day Hawaii Hiking Odyssey takes participants to Kauai's dramatic Na Pali Coast Trail, to Kokee State Park and Waimea Canyon, to visit the island of Molokai, once a leper colony, and to share a 'luau' celebration with a Hawaiian family.

Price includes:

Accommodations, all meals except for one dinner, transportation, activities, guides, inter-island airfare.

Sample trips:

$950 for five days of whale watching.
$995 for seven-day Earth, Fire & Sea trip.
$1,295 for ten-day Hiking Odyssey.

"The best things I liked were the many out-of-the-way places that we saw, with spectacular scenery and excellent discussions of the history and current day sociological issues," commented a participant from Missouri.

FIELD GUIDES INC.

Address: PO Box 160723
Austin TX 78716
Phone: (512)327-4953
Fax: (512)327-9231
Contact: Allan Griffith, Business Manager

Bird-lovers enjoy these tours run by professional birding experts through Field Guides Inc. of Texas. They're planned to coincide with peak times for spotting species, and the schedules allow plenty of time to look for them at a leisurely pace. There are also opportunities to enjoy the other wildlife and natural beauty of the regions visited. Most days are spent in the field, often starting before dawn to reach birding areas when song and activity are at their height. There are also some nighttime excursions to see nocturnal birds.

In Alaska, travelers tour the Pribolof Islands, Denali National Park, Barrow, Kenai Fjords National Park, and Anchorage; they may see Harlequin Ducks, Three-toed Woodpeckers, and Northern Hawk Owls, among scores of others.

In Arizona, amid the Sonoroan Desert Plains they look for Gray Hawks, Mexican Chickadees, Red-faced Warblers, and the Elegant Trogon in the summer heat. There's a trip to Cape May, New Jersey in October to watch the annual migration; to Klamath Basin, California in February for the largest winter gathering of Bald Eagles; and to Durbin, West Virginia in June to explore the spruce bogs in the Allegheny Mountains, where hundreds of birds breed every year.

Trips abroad include explorations of Guatemala, Costa Rica, China, Australia, Papua New Guina, Ecuador, Brazil, Chile, the Antarctic islands, and Bolivia.

Group size is limited to about 15 participants, with two guides. Travelers usually stay in comfortable, modern hotels, except in areas where birding sites are far away from such amenities when they stay in country inns or tent camps. Good binoculars are essential.

Price includes:

Accommodations, meals, transportation, entrance fees for parks, tips, guide services.

Sample trips:

$445 for weekend in Cape May, NJ.
$1,495 for 10 days in N.E. Mexico.
$2,495 for 10 days in Alaska.
$4,185 for 26 days in Kenya.

FOLKWAYS INSTITUTE/TRAVEL

Address: **14600 S E Aldridge Road**
Portland OR 97236-6518
Phone: **(503)658-6600**
Fax: **(503)658-8672**
Contact: **Lois Mack, Program Director**

"We believe that an individual's growth in understanding global relationships requires a prepared, personal encounter with various nationalities and the environments which mold their culture," notes Folkways Executive Director David Christopher. "Our commitment to cross-cultural education goes beyond a token country visit with experiential learning."

The Institute's travel programs focus on specific issues. The tour of New Zealand visits early education centers observing classes of grades 1 to 3 in New Zealand schools; the emphasis is on literacy and bilingual education and includes Maori schools. Photography workshops examine the people and landscapes of Nepal, Thailand, Australia, and Mexico. There's a culinary tour of China, on which participants taste the regional cuisines of Fuzhou, Shanghai, Suzhou, Beijing, and Chengdu and visit farms, fishing villages, farmers markets, and street bazaars. And travelers to Peru tour traditional weaving centers and join celebrations of the fiesta in Paucartambo.

There's an Elderhostel program in Nepal at the Cultural Heritage Center in Kathmandu to study the language, family structure, history, and arts of the region. In Kenya, the program is led by the Planetarium Director and Instructor in astronomy at Oregon's Mt. Hood Community College and focuses on the night skies. In Egypt, participants tour the pyramids, visit with the Christian minority of Coptic Egypt, and learn about the culture of Islam and the life of the modern state.

Price includes:

Accommodations, meals, transportation, guides, lectures, excursions, park fees.

Sample trips:

$2,980 for three weeks in Kenya.
$3,140 for 16 days in Egypt.
$3,155 for three weeks culinary tour of China.

FOUNDATION FOR AMERICAN-CHINESE CULTURAL EXCHANGES

Address: **475 Riverside Drive/Suite 245**
New York NY 10115
Phone: **(212)870-2525**
Fax: **(212)749-0397**
Contact: **Robert Dodds, Program Director**

Established in 1980, the Foundation is a nonprofit, apolitical, independent organization working to facilitate the exchange of cultural traditions and ideas between Americans and Chinese.

FACCE organizes art exhibits, film screenings, trade conferences, lectures and two Summer Chinese Learning Programs—the Language and Culture program, and the Trade and Law program. A total of 429 people have participated since 1980, with most students aged 21 to 28. The courses are recognized by American colleges and universities for credit.

The Language and Culture program offers intensive Mandarin Chinese instruction in Shanghai, Nanjing, and Changchun. Each course is the equivalent of one academic year in Chinese. Classes are small and are geared to all levels of ability. There are 20 hours a week of classes, taught by native Mandarin speakers, and students spend a great deal of time on homework and preparation. Outside activities include theater, films, and opera as well as visits to museums, temples, and Chinese musical performances, plus a few overnight excursions.

"Students are given a high degree of independence and are urged to explore the city on their own," notes a staff member.

The Trade and Law program is primarily a lecture course, with Chinese and Western experts addressing the issues of foreign trade and the relevant laws. The program is geared to college students and graduates with a background in business, law, or Chinese studies. Some knowledge of the language is helpful, but not essential, and language tutorials can be arranged. The program includes meetings with Americans working in Chinese foreign trade and field trips to trade institutions, factories, the courts, and financial centers, including an optional visit to Taiwan.

Price includes:

Accommodations, tuition, all meals, excursions, activities. FACCE can make air travel arrangements.

Sample trips:

$2,898 for eight weeks Language and Culture program.
$3,500 for eight weeks Trade and Law program.

FOUNDATION FOR FIELD RESEARCH

Address: **PO Box 2010**
Alpine CA 92001
Phone: **(619)445-9264**
Contact: **Thomas Banks**

Founded in 1982, the Foundation coordinates research expeditions by finding willing volunteers from the general public to work as field assistants to scientists conducting research around the world. The researchers send the Foundation their projects, which are carefully analyzed and reviewed. If accepted, the research work is described in the newsletter sent out to Foundation members who sign up for projects that interest them.

These include studies of pre-Columbian textiles in Peru; the effect of tourists on the whales in the St. Lawrence River in Canada; the survival of giant leather turtles of Michoacan, Mexico; tool use among chimpanzees in Liberia; and the history of an ancient volcanic caldera (crater) in Big Bend, Texas.

Some projects last a few days, some weeks, and some a month. Volunteers range in age from 14 to 86, and include doctors, students, teachers, managers, secretaries, factory workers, librarians, attorneys and retirees. They are always actively involved with the work.

Price includes:

All volunteers make a tax-deductible contribution toward expedition costs which covers lodging, all meals, transportation during the expedition, field gear, and preparatory booklet.

Sample trips:

$475 for five days, turtle project, Michoacan.
$1,215 for two weeks archaeology project, Ireland.
$1,325 for 16 days in Liberia studying primates.

One participant noted:"I was encouraged and allowed to do as much as I wished, so that I learned from hands-on experience about all phases of the excavation. Never a dull moment!"

FRENCH-AMERICAN EXCHANGE

Address: **313 C Street NE**
Washington DC 20002
Phone: **(202)546-9612**
Contact: **James Pondolfino**

Summer courses and academic-year-abroad programs are offered by the French-American Exchange in Montpellier, France.

The summer courses, organized in collaboration with ILP-ARC Langues Institute, emphasize the aural method of instruction. This technique is designed to condition your ear to the language, and is based on the theory that the ability to learn a foreign language is directly related to a person's ability to hear the language. The school has language labs equipped with equalizers and acoustic shells "which enable a progressive re-education of the ear, improving memorization and reproduction of sounds."

Classes run for two, four or eight 8 weeks and meet Monday through Friday for three hours every morning. Daily lab work is required. There are courses on art history, French literature, and French movies in the afternoons. Students stay in dorm rooms, hotels or apartments, or live with a French family.

Semester and academic-year-abroad programs also offer special courses for foreigners at the Institut des Etudiants Etrangers,. Students may be able to go to some regular classes at the Universite Paul Valery in Montpellier.

Price includes:

Accommodations, meals, transportation, optional orientation in Paris, tuition, administrative fee.

Sample courses:

$2,067 for four weeks in summer program.
$3,320 for eight weeks in summer program.
$3,800 for one semester.
$6,320 for October-June, academic year abroad.

GEORGE WASHINGTON UNIVERSITY

Address: **American Studies Program**
Anthropology Department/P 203B
Washington DC 20052
Phone: **(202)994-6073**
Contact: **Bernard Mergen, Professor of American Civilization.**

Every summer since 1976, a group of undergraduates and graduate students interested in Mesoamerican archaeology and history has traveled to Mayan and Colonial sites in Mexico and Belize.

For three weeks they examine "ancient and modern Maya culture from an interdisciplinary perspective" and explore "the relationships among art, ecology, architecture, and sociopolitical systems," as Professor Mergen explains.

Before leaving for the sites, students read *The Maya* by Michael Coe, *The Caste War of Yucatan* by Nelson Reed, and selections from Bernal Diaz del Castillo's *The Discovery and Conquest of Mexico.* They keep academic diaries in the field.

Price includes:

Airfare from Washington DC, accommodations in hotels, meals, site fees, transportation, instructors, interpreter, travel agent.

Sample trip:

$1,500 for three weeks.

GERHARD'S BICYCLE ODYSSEYS

Address: **4949 SW Macadam Avenue**
Portland OR 97201
Phone: **(503)223-2402**
Fax: **(503)224-6320**
Contact: **Gerhard Meng**

Gerhard Meng was born in Germany and has traveled widely. Since 1974, he's been taking Americans on his carefully planned bicycle tours in Norway, Luxembourg, Germany, France, Austria, and France aimed at showing travelers a unique view of Europe. Bikers stay in first-class hotels, country inns, or castles, chosen for the high quality of the services and the location. Good food is an essential part of the trip.

In Norway, there's also a cruise along fjords and a stop at a 13th century farmhouse. In Austria, bikers arrive in time for the Munich Oktoberfest, with its procession and parties, and later spend two days exploring Vienna.

Biking distances offer choices for different levels of bikers, and routes follow country lanes away from the tourist roads. No group has more than 20 adults, who usually range in age from 25 to 60, about half of them single. Two multilingual tour leaders accompany every trip.

Price includes:

Accommodations, meals, transportation, sightseeing, daily outline, map of route.

Sample trips:

$1,295 for eight nights in Luxembourg and Germany.
$1,995 for 14 nights in Brittany, France.
$2,295 for 14 nights in Norway.

One participant noted, "I suspect you run the Mercedes of bike tours. If I had the time and money, I would go on one or two Odyssey tours each year."

GLICKMAN-POPKIN BASSOON CAMP

Address: **740 Arbor Road**
Winston-Salem NC 27104
Phone: **(919)725-5681**
Contact: **Mark A. Popkin**

This one-week music camp run every summer by professional bassoonists Loren Glickman and Mark Popkin is designed for musicians over the age of 18. In the beautiful setting of Wildacres, a magnificent mountaintop retreat of 1,400 acres near Little Switzerland in the Blue Ridge Mountains, about 100 bassoonists of all ages and stages come together to study, practice, and perform. This year, there is also a second one-week session at Emerald Isle, described as a "Bassoon Camp By the Sea" run by Mark Popkin.

On acceptance, students are assigned music to prepare. At camp, they attend lectures, practice, rehearse, and perform as soloists and in ensembles. Daily master classes by Loren Glickman and Mark Popkin are offered to advanced and intermediate students.

Also in attendance are visiting guest musicians, experts on bassoon repair and restoration, a representative of a bassoon manufacturing company, and an ever-ready accompanist. The Double Reed Shop sells music.

Mark Popkin has worked with the New York City Center Opera and Ballet, the New Jersey and Houston Symphony Orchestras, the Casals Festival, and the Mostly Mozart Festival, among others. He is on the faculty of the North Carolina School of the Arts.

Loren Glickman has performed as a soloist with the Chamber Music Society of Lincoln Center and the Casals Festival. He is currently on the faculties of Queens College, City University of New York, and the Juilliard School of Music.

Price includes:

Accommodations, all meals, instruction. A few scholarships available.

Sample Courses:

$360 for one week at Wildacres.
$245 a week for non-participating spouses.

HAZAN MASTER CLASSES IN ITALIAN COOKING

Address: **PO Box 285, Circleville NY 10919**
Phone: **(914)692-7104**
Contact: **Susan Cox**

Marcella Hazan is the author of *The Classic Italian Cook Book, More Classic Italian Cooking* and *Marcella's Italian Kitchen.* Her husband Victor is the author of *Italian Wine.* Several times a year, the couple open their home in Italy atop a 16th century palazzo to a group of six students interested in learning about Italian cooking and Italian wine.

The Hazan Master Class ranges over a wide variety of topics in an atmosphere of intimate informality. On the first day, students visit the historic produce and fish market in the nearby Rialto and enjoy a banquet at one of the best Venetian restaurants. For the next five days there is instruction for several hours daily as students prepare different dishes, followed by a leisurely meal accompanied by wine from Victor's private cellar.

Due to the popularity of this class, reservations are accepted two years in advance. Students send a refundable deposit of $200 with applications and are told when the first date becomes available.

For the first time, a separate Baking Workshop in Bologna is offered this year, taught by Margherita Simili, who has worked with Marcella Hazan for 12 years. Margherita and her sister Valeria owned and operated Bologna's most highly regarded bakery which they have just sold, and are now teaching others the secrets of their success. The workshop curriculum was developed with Marcella Hazan, and includes Apulian olive bread, Tuscan bread, farmhouse bread, cheese tortes in bread crust, hand-pulled grissini, and baker's style pizza.

Price includes:

Tuition only.

Sample courses:

$1,500 for week's course with Marcella and Victor Hazan.
$1,200 for week's Baking Workshop in Bologna.

HEARTWOOD OWNER-BUILDER SCHOOL

Address: **Johnson Hill Road**
Washington MA 01235
Phone: **(413)623-6677**
Contact: **Will Beemer**

Want to build your own house? Will and Michele Beemer of the Heartwood School in the Berkshire Hills can show you how. "Heartwood was established in 1978 to teach the skills and knowledge it takes to build an energy-efficient house," Beemer explains. "The determination to become an active creator of your environment claims back your right to make a difference."

The school's approach is that "the best way to learn something is to *do* it," so students spend time in the classroom studying house mock-ups and models and then go and work at what they've learned: framing wall sections, calculating beam sizes, laying out a house foundation, orienting for solar exposure, etc.

The three-week course focuses on the basic information, and there are also one-week courses on related building topics. The staff are all licensed building contractors. Guest faculty include carpenters, a mason and stone carver, and an expert in timber frame construction.

Usually about 15 people take the house-building course, offered four times a year, including teachers, truck drivers, architects, social workers, retirees, high school students and others. The programs are geared to both skilled builders and beginners.

Price includes:

Tuition and lunches. A list of housing options in Washington is provided.

Sample trips:

$325 for a one-week course.
$700 per person for three-week course.
$1,200 for couple for three-week course.

A social worker from New York praised, "The accepting, patient attitude on the part of the staff, who were very knowledgeable about construction and cared to teach the students to do good work. The experience has definitely enhanced my feeling of self-sufficiency."

HIGH ADVENTURE TOURS

Address: 4000 Massachusetts Avenue NW
Suite 1426
Washington DC 20016
Phone: (202)686-0023
Contact: Shirley M. Duncan

Since 1978, Shirley Duncan has led groups of Americans on tours to remote, unspoiled, culturally fascinating areas of the world. These include Syria, Yemen, Cyprus, and Jordan. Travelers meet the people, visit homes, and spend time sightseeing in museums and historic sites. Every trip has a knowledgeable local guide as well as lectures and discussions along the way.

"There's no trekking or roughing it," Shirley Duncan explained. "Group members are well-traveled, interesting people. Our tours combine comfort with the adventure and excitement of off-the-beaten-path travel."

In Syria the group visits Ugarit, the site of the world's first alphabet, tour Crusader castles from medieval times, and explore the bazaars of Aleppo and Damascus.

In Jordan, participants travel to Petra, the fabulous "Lost City" carved out of pink cliffs 2,500 years ago; Mount Nebo where Moses looked out on the Promised Land; and Jerash, with its magnificent Roman ruins. In North Yemen, they see veiled women and men in robes wearing daggers in the streets, the remains of the Queen of Sheba's palace, and the old coffee ports of Mocha.

Price includes:

Airfare from New York, accommodations, buses, most meals, sightseeing, guides, escort.

Sample trips:

$3,525 for 18 days in Syria and Petra.
$4,340 for 16 days in Petra and Yemen.
$5,950 for 26 days in Syria, Petra, and Yemen.

HUGH GLASS BACKPACKING COMPANY

Address: **PO Box 110796**
Anchorage AK 99511
Phone: **(907)344-1340**
Contact: **Chuck Ash**

High-quality adventures led by experienced Alaskan guides into some of the finest wilderness in North America are the specialty of this outdoor company. Group size is limited to six people to enhance the experience and reduce the impact on the environment. Participants travel in aluminum canoes, rafts, and Klepper kayaks as well as hiking and backpacking.

Kayak trips paddle through the Kenai Fjords National Park, and Katmai National Park; raft trips explore the Arctic National Wildlife Refuge. There are backpacking treks in June into the Refuge to spot the migration of the caribou, bears, and wolves, among other wild animals, as well as a trek through the Chugach Mountains.

"The physical demands vary from trip to trip," a staff member notes, "with the most strenuous being backpacking. If you lead an active lifestyle or do some pre-trip training you will be able to participate easily."

There are wilderness fishing adventures to Bristol Bay and along the outer Kenai coast, for both spin and fly fishermen.

Price includes:

Accommodations, transportation, meals, medical kit, pre-trip literature, guiding, advisory services. Rental gear available.

Sample trips:

$495 for five-day trek in Chugach Mountains.
$995 for one week/July kayak in Kenai Fjords Park.
$1,875 for 10-day raft trip to Arctic Refuge.

HUMANITIES INSTITUTE, THE

Address: **PO Box 18-BP**
Belmont MA 02178
Phone: **(617)484-3191/(800)327-1657**
Fax: **(617)484-5612**
Contact: **Martha Mueller Ph.D., Director**

"If you love travel, but not superficial tours that are long on transportation but short on thought, or if you're wary of traveling on your own, or you want a group experience that allows plenty of time for personal exploration, we may have the ideal travel and learning program for you," declares Martha Mueller, Director of The Humanities Institute.

The Institute, founded in 1975 by Dr. William R. Mueller, her father, sponsors year-round educational and cultural programs in England, Ireland, Australia, New Zealand, Greece, Italy, France, Eastern Europe, Russia, Canada, Israel, and Japan. In the United States, there are programs in New England in the fall, in New Orleans in the spring and a program in New York City at Christmas. There is also a winter program in Puerto Rico.

The Institute works in conjunction with the University of North Carolina at Greensboro, Lesley College in Cambridge, Massachusetts, and the School of Continuing Studies, University of Toronto.

In England, travel seminars are offered at Cambridge University on drama, art, architecture, and contemporary British writing. There's a walking tour through Wordsworth's Lake District, and in Edinburgh, classes on the Scottish literary tradition and 18th century Scotland. In Australia, the focus is on education and literacy, with tours of Sydney, Canberra, Armidale and Brisbane. In Greece, Dimitris Gounelas, lecturer in modern Greek literature at the University of Thessaloniki, explains Greek literature and takes student to historic sites. Another tour explores Japan's arts and culture.

Price includes:

Accommodations, some meals, excursions, lectures. Airfare not included but group rate available.

Sample trips:

$1,150 for six days walking in Lake District.
$2,600 for 18 days in Greece.
$3,150 for 20 days in Australia.

A participant from Chicago praised the "rich and invigorating program, offering so many different kinds of experiences with congenial people who share my interests... A sure antidote for burn-out!"

INSTITUTE OF CHINA STUDIES

Address: 7341 North Kolmar Street
Lincolnwood IL 60646
Phone: (312)677-0987
Fax: (312)673-2634
Contact: Harry Kiang

The Institute of China Studies is a nonprofit organization which sponsors tours to China and Chinese-language courses in Shanghai, publishes books, and conducts festivals and seminars.

The 21-day summer tour of China visits Hangzhou, Suzhou, Nanjing, the Yangtze river, the mausoleum of Emperor Qin Shi Huang, Quilin, and Xian and includes attendance at the International Geographical Union conference in Beijing.

The summer Chinese language courses are held at Shanghai University and Shanghai Teachers University. There are classes in basic Chinese, reading and listening comprehension, calligraphy, and composition as well as lectures on Chinese history, culture, language arts, cuisine, music, dance, archeology, and more. The programs run for four to six weeks, followed by a ten-day tour of China.

The fall and winter programs offer semester stays of several months, beginning in September and in March, and include language classes and visits to factories, homes, schools, theaters, and the countryside.

Price includes:

Airfare from west coast, accommodations, most meals, transportation, transfers, sightseeing, events, tuition, guides.

Sample trips:

$3,100 for 21-day tour of China.
$2,500 for four weeks Summer Study; $500 for 10-day tour.
$4,000 for five-month semester (no airfare).

INTERHOSTEL

Address: University of New Hampshire
Division of Continuing Education
6 Garrison Avenue
Durham NH 03824
Phone: (603)862-1147/(800)733-9753
Fax: (603)862-1113
Contact: Sue Crosby, Program Coordinator

Described as "an international educational experience for active adults over 50," Interhostel, founded in 1980, offers mature travelers a unique opportunity to learn about foreign cultures.

Participants are hosted by an overseas university, college, or cultural institution and enjoy daily lectures, seminars, field trips, and excursions led by professors and local experts. There are also social meetings with residents and entertainment.

A typical day begins with breakfast in the faculty club, followed by a class in conversational language of the country, a lecture on its historical origins and cultural influences, and lunch on the patio of the city's art museum. The afternoon will be spent in seminars. In the evening, dinner is served at the faculty club. Afterward, there's a reception with members of the university and an outing to the symphony or theater.

Interhostel offers programs year-round in England, France, Germany, Greece, Ireland, Portugal, Puerto Rico, Scotland, Sweden, and Switzerland, and recently has added Australia, Austria, China, Costa Rica, Holland, Italy, Thailand, and Russia.

Price includes:

Accommodations, all meals, airport transfers, transportation, tuition, activities, admission fees, guides, escort. Airfare not included but travel arrangements must be made through Interhostel travel agent.

Sample trips:

$1,295 for 19 days at University of Puerto Rico.
$1,325 for 17 days at Hangzhou University, China.
$1,750 for 20 days at University of Canterbury, N.Z.

"What you get through Interhostel is more than travel," noted one participant, "it opens your eyes to a country through a deeper understanding of its people and culture." And a woman commented: "No more boring group tours full of sleepy tourists... participants are the kind of people you want to share things with long afterwards!"

INTERNATIONAL ALPINE SCHOOL

Address: **Box 3037**
Eldorado Springs CO 80025
Phone: **(303)494-4904**
Contact: **Sandy East, Director**

The International Alpine School, founded in 1968, is recognized as one of the best climbing schools for those who are serious about learning the technical skills needed for safe rock climbing, ice climbing, and skiing. Instructional programs last from three to 24 days. All IAS guides have at least ten years of world-wide climbing experience. IAS also offers guide training programs.

In conjunction with the Winter Park Handicap Competition Program, IAS runs a class teaching blind people rock climbing techniques and plans to organize a major mountaineering expedition for them. The company also offers Avalanche Seminars on how to evaluate snowpack conditions and recognize when they're dangerous.

In summer, there are week-long climbing classes in Colorado's Sangre De Cristo peaks, soaring over 14,000 feet high. In winter, programs are based in Ouray, Colorado, where students scale frozen waterfalls. While most programs are based in Colorado, there are occasional expeditions to Alaska's Mount McKinley, the Himalayas, the French and Swiss Alps, and the Andes in Peru, Chile and Argentina.

Price includes:

All instruction, food, cooking gear, tents, technical climbing gear. Sleeping bags, boots, ice axes, and hammers can be rented.

Sample trips:

$125 for three-day rock climbing, Colorado.
$580 for five-day summer/winter mountaineering, Colorado.
$1,675 for 14-day ski tour in Los Andes, Chile.
$2,495 for 25 days climbing in Himalayas, Nepal.

INTERNATIONAL BICYCLE TOURS

Address: **12 Mid Place**
Chappaqua NY 10514
Phone: **(914)238-4576**
Fax: **(914)238-4573**
Contact: **Frank Behrendt, Director**

A native of Amsterdam, Frank Behrendt has led bike trips around the world since 1976. He and his trained leaders take bikers across Holland for a spring tulip tour and summer and fall tours. Other trips travel through France, England, Russia, and China. Every tour has two multilingual guides whose skills include a thorough knowledge of the area as well as the ability to fix flat tires.

"Careful planning ensures that our tours are leisurely excursions, never athletic marathons," Behrendt explains. "We always start our tours at a leisurely pace and slowly add a bit of mileage as you get used to the cycling."

There's a support van to carry luggage and bike equipment and plenty of stops for snacks and picture-taking. The tours are ideal for families as well as for individuals, and children are welcome. IBT also specializes in tours for travelers over 60. Some participants have cycled extensively and some not for many years.

Price includes:

Accommodations, group transportation from airport, bicycle, T-shirt, breakfast and dinner daily, tips, taxes.

Sample trips:

$1,100 for one-week Tulip Tour of Holland.
$1,530 for two-week tour of France.
$2,300 for two-week tour of Russia (with all meals).

INTERNATIONAL COUNCIL FOR CULTURAL EXCHANGE, INC.

Address: **1559 Rockville Pike**
Rockville MD 20852
Phone: **(301)983-9479**
Fax: **(301)770-4499**
Contact: **Stanley Salsberg, Registrar**

ICCE is a nonprofit cultural exchange organization, founded in 1982, offering campus, home stay, and hotel accommodations in France, Italy, and Spain for travelers studying art, language, and music while on vacation.

ICCE also advises individuals on where to study abroad, depending on their particular needs.

Summer programs in France are held on a university campus on the French Riviera overlooking the Bay of Angels and its beautiful beach. Courses run for two, three or four weeks, and classes are held for about four hours every morning. There are supplementary cultural lectures by French and American professors and specialists and French conversation classes in the afternoons.

Outside activities include theater, movies, swimming, dances, fetes, and beach parties. Meals are served at the student cafeteria. ICEE also organizes weekend sightseeing excursions.

The Italian program is at the Center for International Studies, Collegio Colombo in Viareggio, a beach resort and seaport on the west coast of Tuscany, about fifty miles from Florence. Students live on campus in a villa a few minutes' walk from the beach and the town center. There are gardens, tennis courts, and sports facilities and a dining room serving Italian cuisine.

"People join our program to have an experience of immersion in the culture," noted a program coordinator. "They're not getting the Americanized version of the location."

Price includes:

Airfare, accommodations, most meals, tuition, sightseeing, activities. orientation, events, guides.

Sample trips:

$2,098 for three weeks in Italy.
$2,398 for four weeks in France.

INTERNATIONAL TRAVEL STUDY

Address: **5700 4th Street North**
St. Petersburg FL 33703
Phone: **(813)525-2096**
Contact: **Jim Hyland**

More than 70,000 students and teachers have traveled with ITS all over the world. The affiliated offices in Paris, Madrid, Athens, Rome, Switzerland, and Germany are under the supervision of the ITS London office. The company assigns bilingual personnelto the European campuses to assist participants.

Groups of no more than 40 students travel together on ITS tours. They stay in hotels with private baths, tour in air conditioned buses, and there is strong emphasis on the educational aspects of the trip.

The European tour includes Rothenburg and Munich in Germany, the Italian Tyrol; a week's cruise of the Greek Islands; and stops in Venice, Florence, Rome, Switzerland, Paris and London. The tour to Russia from Miami includes trips to Moscow and Leningrad and returns via Ireland, Wales, and a week in England.

Price includes:

Airfare, accommodations, transportation, most meals, excursions, events, transfers, taxes, tips, guides, escorts.

Sample trips:

$2,299 for 18 days in Russia and the British Isles.
$2,799 for 22 days of European Adventure.

INTERNATIONAL ZOOLOGICAL EXPEDITIONS INC.

Address: **210 Washington Street**
Sherborn MA 01770
Phone: **(508)655-1461**
Contact: **Fred Dodd**

"Each year thousands vacation in Belize, but only a handful do it right," states Fred Dodd. "We handle the handful."

With over 20 years of continuous operation, the company considers itself the most experienced nature research/tour company in Belize and offers a high level of expertise on all its expeditions. The trips include birding, nature study, and exploration of the barrier reef and tropical rain forest.

The IZE excursions in Belize, a small country bordering Mexico's Yucatan Peninsula and roughly the size of Massachusetts, run from December through August. They are often organized for university research groups and accompanied by experts in science, archeology, wildlife, and marine biology.

IZE's field stations are set on a barrier reef and in the remote primary rain forests of the interior. Guides lead participants to hidden waterfalls, uncharted caves, beautiful climax forests laden with orchids and bromeliads, sea-bird rookeries, mangrove swamps, and the thatched huts of the Kekchi and Maya Indians.

There is excellent fishing. The Belize Barrier Reef offers spectacular scuba diving and snorkeling. And there's an annual August Herpetology Expedition collecting and photographing snakes, including boa constrictors. Less active explorers can rent one of the simple cottages on a deserted coral reef island, with a cook, maid, and all meals provided.

Price includes:

Accommodations, meals, transportation, guides, boats, lectures and transfers.

Sample trips:

$375 for 10 days at biological field station.
$1,000 for tour of Belize with charter air and hotels.

ISLAND BICYCLE ADVENTURES

Address: 569 Kapahulu Avenue
Honolulu HI 96815
Phone: (808)734-0700/(800)233-2226
Contact: Roberta Baker, Tour Director

The company offers bike tours of the Hawaiian islands led by people who take a special course on interpreting Hawaii and who love to share their knowledge of the geology, volcanoes, flora, and fauna of this unique environment.

On Kauai, you start from Lihue Airport and explore Kokee State Park, Waimea Canyon, and the Na Pali coast. The Maui Island tour includes a hike into the extinct volcanic crater of Mount Haleakala. The Hawaii tour visits coffee and macadamia nut plantations as well as Kealakekua Bay, where Captain Cook was killed.

All the tours run for six days, and are arranged so that they can be combined. Accommodation varies from modern resorts to old style family hotels. A support van travels with the group.

Price includes:

Accommodations, all meals, maps, route description, complimentary water bottle and helmet during tour. Bikes are available for rental at $79 per tour.

Sample trips:

$785 for one-week tour.
$1,570 for two tours; includes inter-island airfare.

JOURNEYS INTERNATIONAL INC.

Address: **4011 Jackson Road**
Ann Arbor MI 48103
Phone: **(313)665-4407/(800)255-8735**
Fax: **(313)665-2945**
Contact: **Kathy O'Neal, Operations Director**

The company's goal is to promote nature and culture conservation in the areas it visits. Many of its guides are professionally employed in conservation or local development projects. Founded in 1978, the company offers dozens of international cultural and nature-oriented explorations. These include a trip in the Himalayas designed specially for artists, with visits to local artists along the way. Other Asia journeys explore Everest, Kangchenjunga, Tibet, and Ladakh.

In Africa, there are safaris in Kenya and Tanzania and a climb of Mt. Kilimanjaro. In South America, participants trek in the Andes. In Ecuador, travelers cruise the Galapagos Islands, or choose to climb the volcanoes. And in Costa Rica, participants visit Tortuguero National Park, the Monteverde Cloud Forest, and the Marenco Biological Station. Other trips go to Mexico, Argentina, Alaska, Hawaii, Madagascar, Papua New Guinea, and more.

"Many participants often travel alone and don't need the security of luxury accommodations and a large group," notes a staff member. "Our groups allow like-minded independent travelers to combine resources in completing a trip unavailable or unaffordable to most individuals." Groups range from six to 12 people.

Part of the cost of each trip goes to the Earth Preservation Fund, a nonprofit organization that encourages staff and travelers to volunteer their time and resources to help local communities protect their natural and cultural heritage. Projects include distributing vegetable seeds and forestry seedlings to villages in Nepal, working with local schools in conservation education, and supporting preservation and reconstruction of monasteries in destination countries.

Price includes:

Accommodations, most meals, permits, equipment, guides. Airfare not included but group fares can be arranged.

Sample trips:

$995 for 16-day Annapurna Family Trek, Nepal.
$1,295 for 11-day Hawaii Hiking Odyssey.
$1,595 for 24-day Kashmir-Ladakh Cultural Trek.
$2,395 for 16-day Japan Cultural Odyssey.

KENTUCKY INSTITUTE FOR EUROPEAN STUDIES

Address: **Murray State University**
Murray KY 42071
Phone: **(502)762-3091**
Fax: **(502)762-3434**
Contact: **J. Milton Grimes, Director**

The Kentucky Institute for European Studies is a consortium of eight universities—Murray State, Eastern Kentucky, Western Kentucky, Morehead State, Northern Kentucky, the University of Kentucky, Berea College, and Union College. Founded in 1975, the Institute operates summer programs in Austria, France, Spain, Italy, and Germany, designed to help American students gain fluency in a foreign language and understand the history, politics, and culture of Europe.

In France, students study in Paris and Nimes. The French program includes conversation, composition, and literature, as well as courses in business law and French culture.

In Madrid, Spain, the program includes Spanish-language classes and seminars on art, painting, international finance, and marketing. And in Salzburg and Bregenz, Austria, the program emphasizes music, with voice and piano instruction and courses on instrumental music of the classical and romantic periods.

Price includes:

Airfare, accommodations, some meals, student ID card, tuition, excursions, cultural events.

Sample trips:

$2,145 for five weeks in Salzburg, Austria.
$2,650 for five weeks in Florence, Italy.
$2,869 for six weeks in France.

KIBBUTZ ALIYA DESK

Address: **27 West 20 Street, 9th Floor**
New York NY 10011
Phone: **(212)255-1138/(800)444-7007**
Fax: **(212)929-3459**
Contact: **Director**

The kibbutz, a collective farm, is a unique Israeli creation. In 1909, the first kibbutz, Degania, was established by 24 young people from Russia who began to farm a small plot of land on the shores of the Sea of Galilee. They chose to live by idealistic principles of sharing all the work and the profits and losses equally among themselves. Today, there are hundreds of such farms in Israel. Although they have changed over the years, the concept of communal ownership has survived.

Kibbutz Aliya Desk offers several work/study programs for Americans who want to spend time on a kibbutz. The programs last several months, six days a week. There are Semester

Kibbutz and University programs, where students work on a kibbutz and spend time taking courses at a university in Haifa or Jerusalem.

For those with less time, there are Kibbutz Summer Ulpan Programs of four to eight weeks work, with some study, followed by a week touring the country. Others can volunteer to work on the kibbutz for at least one month in exchange for free room and board.

Price includes:

Airfare, accommodations, meals, transportation, tuition.

Sample trips:

$65 for four weeks, volunteer(no airfare or insurance).
$1,560 for eight weeks Summer Ulpan.
$3,290 for fall semester, Kibbutz/University plus dorm.

KOSCIUSZKO FOUNDATION

Address: **15 East 65 Street**
New York NY 10021-6595
Phone: **(212)734-2130**
Fax: **(212)628-4552**
Contact: **Monika A. Olszer**

The Foundation was created in 1925 to improve the understanding of Poland and Polish culture, history, and traditions among Americans, as well as encouraging the study of the Polish language and heritage among those of Polish ancestry.

Every summer, the Foundation organizes several programs in Poland. At the Jagiellonian University in Cracow in southern Poland, an intensive Polish-language course is offered as well as seminars on such topics as Polish art and the role of the Catholic Church in Poland.

Similar programs are offered at the Catholic University of Lublin, at Lublin's Marie Curie-Sklodowska University, and at the University of Warsaw. And Adam Mickiewicz University in Poznan, the trade center, offers courses on Polish economics, foreign trade, and social-political issues.

Students live in dorms, with shared toilet and bathing facilities, and take their meals in student dining halls. The Foundation warns participants to be prepared for a great deal of walking to classes and stair climbing, since there are no elevators.

Price includes:

Accommodations, all meals, tuition, excursions and cultural activities.

Sample trips:

$450 for three weeks in Warsaw.
$625 for four weeks in Cracow.
$750 for six weeks in Lublin.

LANGUAGE STUDIES ENROLLMENT CENTER

Address: **PO Box 5095**
Anaheim CA 92814
Phone: **(714)527-2918**
Telex: **91025 08276 LSEC UQ**
Contact: **Bill Fagan**

"Language - Key to Global Understanding" is the motto of the Language Studies Enrollment Center.

Since 1974, it has arranged for hundreds of American students to study in Spanish-language and Latin American programs in the Academia Hispano Americana in San Miguel de Allende, Mexico.

Sessions run for four weeks, year-round, with a one week break at the end of December. Every day, there are a couple of hours of oral class work, an hour of pronunciation and practice, an hour of conversation, and several hours of seminars taught in Spanish. Students are tested to find their level before being placed in a class.

San Muguel de Allende is a charming 16th century town, preserved by the Mexican government as a national monument. Built on the side of a hill 6,400 feet above sea level, it has cobbled streets, old stone houses with heavy wooden doors, flowering gardens, shaded patios, and an unusual pink parish church in the center of town, facing the public gardens.

Many students live with Mexican families, although apartments and houses are available for rental, and there are several reasonably priced hotels.

LSEC also organizes four week homestay and language programs in Spain, Costa Rica, Brazil, Portugal, Italy, Germany, Japan, Canada and France.

Price includes:

Tuition only. Accommodation and all meals with a Mexican family is $270 a month.

Sample costs:

$80 tuition for one week.
$300 tuition for four weeks.
$800 tuition for 12 weeks.

LA SABRANENQUE

Address: **217 High Park Boulevard**
Buffalo NY 14226
Phone: **(716)836-8698**
Contact: **Jacqueline C. Simon**

There are two separate programs under the aegis of La Sabranenque, a nonprofit association that has been working since 1969 with volunteers in southern France on projects aimed toward the preservation, restoration, and revitalization of villages, simple monuments, and rural sites.

1) Volunteer Restoration Project

Volunteers spend two or three weeks in the summer restoring and reconstructing old, often medieval, buildings in abandoned historic Mediterranean villages and discover the pleasure of working together on creative projects. La Sabranenque has completely restored the ancient village in Saint Victor la Coste near Avignon. Volunteers from different countries work on several projects in nearby villages, living in modern village homes in Saint Victor la Coste. There are also three other similar projects in Italy.

No previous experience or language ability is necessary. Traditional building techniques are taught on the job by experienced technicians. These include stone masonry, stone-cutting, carpentry, tiling, paving, and making dry stone walls. Volunteers must be at least 18 years of age, and participants usually represent a variety of ages and professions.

2) French Language Sessions:

An intensive three-month immersion program in French language and culture is offered in the spring and fall in Saint Victor la Coste, through La Sabranenque's Centre International. The curriculum covers the equivalent of a year's study and also offers students the opportunity to enjoy village life. There are discussions with local residents, cultural events, movies, and excursions in the region. A few days are spent helping with village restoration projects. All students must be 18 years of age and have some knowledge of basic French.

Price includes:

Accommodations, meals, training, instruction, course materials, excursions, activities.

Sample trips:

1) Restoration Project: $450 for two weeks in France. $780 for three weeks France/Italy.
2) French Language: $3,450 for three months session.

LA VARENNE COOKING SCHOOL

Address: **Box 25574**
Washington DC 20007
Phone: **(202)337-0073/(800)537-6486**
Contact: **Karen Metz, U.S.Representative**

For those seriously interested in learning about cooking, this cooking school offers a variety of courses in French cuisine held in Paris and Burgundy, France. La Varenne is named after Francois Pierre de la Varenne, one of the most important chefs of the 17th century and author of the first modern French cookbook.

In Burgundy, students live in the luxurious Chateau du Fey 90 miles south of Paris, surrounded by acres of woods, a heated swimming pool, and a walled garden with fruit and vegetables. Here experienced chefs offer week-long courses on several aspects of French cooking, including bistro cooking; entertaining; the regional dishes of Burgundy, Alsace, Provence and the southwest; and the secrets of making French pastry and chocolate. All courses include cooking demonstrations, wine tasting, excursions to nearby vineyards, and dinners in a fine country restaurant.

A special Fall Gastronomic Program in September coincides with the wine harvest and focuses on typical Burgundian dishes.

The program is personally hosted by Anne Willan, La Varenne's founder and president. Anne Willan is the author of *La Varenne Pratique,* among other books, and president of the International Association of Culinary Professionals. She and her husband, Mark Cherniavsky, live in the Chateau du Fey and farm the land.

The Ecole de Cuisine La Varenne in Paris offers a five month course of instruction leading to the Grand Diplome certificate for those who complete the program. Shorter courses are available for those who want to learn particular techniques.

Price includes:

Accommodations, all meals, wines, activities, excursions, facilities, transportation.

Sample courses:

$1,995 for one week in summer in Burgundy.
$2,595 for one week Fall Program in Burgundy.

LOS ANGELES COMMUNITY COLLEGES

Address: **International Education Program**
855 N Vermont Ave., Bung. 129
Los Angeles CA 90029
Phone: **(213)666-4255**
Contact: **Dr. Donald Culton,**
Director, International Programs

There's a wide range of students attending Los Angeles Community Colleges district classes, from high-school students to senior citizens, from teachers working on a bilingual certificate to adults of all ages eager for education and intellectual enrichment.

The International Education Program courses offered abroad include semesters or summer sessions studying French in Paris, Italian in Florence, and Spanish in Mexico or Spain. In Rio de Janeiro, there are language classes in Portuguese; students live at the Brazil-United States Institute, a block from Copacabana Beach. In England, a semester program includes general studies in Cambridge.

Other summer programs travel to Baja's Sea of Cortez to explore marine biology and natural history and to Spain to explore the artistic traditions of Granada, Seville, Cordoba, and Toledo.

Price includes:

Airfare, accommodations, some meals, tuition, excursions, facilities. Add $5 per unit enrollment fee. Non-California residents pay an additional $112 per unit.

Sample trips:

$685 for 11 days in Baja California, Mexico.
$1,800 for four-month semester in Mexico.
$2,165 for four weeks in Rio de Janeiro, Brazil.
$4,495 for three-month semester in Florence, Italy.

MARINE SCIENCES UNDER SAILS

Address: **School of Environmental Education**
PO Box 3994
Hollywood FL 33023
Phone: **(305)983-9015**
Contact: **Ned Webster**

Once upon a time, hundreds of small boats sailed up and down the coast of Florida among the mangrove islands, skimming across the shallows, skirting the turquoise water of the coral reefs, and paddling among the everglades of the peninsula.

Today, Marine Sciences Under Sail, a private nonprofit organization, works to educate people about the life and history of the sea around Florida. It also helps in building replicas of old sailing ships, assists the McKee's Sunken Treasure Museum of marine archaeological artifacts, and has established work-study programs so students can take part in the preservation and repair work.

The most popular activities are hands-on, get-wet programs which take people out in sailboats. Participants learn about the vital role the sea and coastal zone play in their lives and the necessity for protecting these natural resources. School groups are taken on one-day outdoor education programs to Pennekamp Coral Reef State Park in the Florida Keys, Everglades National Park at the tip of Florida's mainland, and the John U. Lloyd State Park in Broward County. There is also a three day field trip to the Boy Scouts of America Sea Base in the Florida Keys.

Adult sea-lovers can take a study cruise on a sailboat for a day, a week, or a couple of weeks. There's plenty of time to snorkel in the clear water and to observe coral patch reefs, turtle grass and mangrove creeks just as those on the small sailboats did a hundred years ago.

But Captain Webster warns it's not luxury living. People have to bring their own food and drink and adjust to the lack of space.

"The ocean is our bathtub, sea water toothbrushing is a distinct shock for the usual oral biota, and you may choose to sleep topside under the stars," he advises.

Price includes:

Accommodations only. You bring food and drink.

Sample trips:

$32 per person with six people for daytime sailing trip.
$40 per person with six people for overnight sail.
$77 per person with two people for overnight sail.

METROPOLITAN MUSEUM OF ART

Address: **c/o Raymond & Whitcomb**
400 Madison Avenue
New York NY 10017
Phone: **(212)759-3960/(800)245-9005**
Contact: **Travel Director**

The Museum offers its members a travel program arranged by a professional travel service. The major emphasis is on cruises aboard comfortable ships with land stops to explore local arts and culture. Tours are always accompanied by experts in the region and are offered year-round.

"The sensible schedule, with occasional days at sea, provides leisure to prepare for visits ashore and for reflection upon the significance of the sights you have seen," states Philippe de Montebello, Director of the Museum.

On the 18-day cruise around South America, participants leave from Miami and visit Buenos Aires to explore the old city, travel to Brazil to tour the Natural History Museum in Joinville and, after a train ride to Paranagua, visit Recife and Rio de Janeiro.

A 12-day cruise through the Red Sea sets sail from Suez and stops at These, Luxor, and Abu Simbel to visit the immense ruins of early Egypt. There's an optional four-day exploration of the Sinai desert.

Several cruises go to Europe to see the historic arts and architecture of Holland, France, Spain, Portugal and Scandinavia. Past excursions have visited the Mediterranean cities of Marseilles, Carcassonne, Barcelona, Granada, and Seville, as well as the ancient ruins of Greece and Turkey.

Price includes:

Airfare, accommodations, all meals, lectures, activities, transfers, porterage. Add $400 tax-deductible gift to the Metropolitan Museum of Art. Prices vary depending on cabin aboard the cruise ship.

Sample trips:

$5,750 for 12 days in Egypt and the Red Sea.
$7,865 for 19 days in Scandinavia.
$10,490 for 18 days in South America.

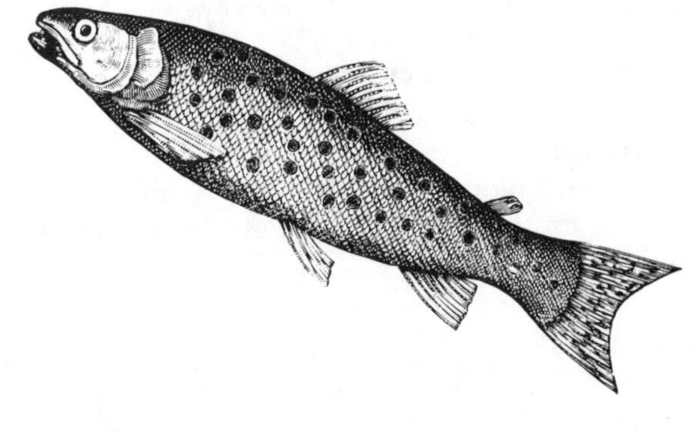

METROPOLITAN OPERA GUILD

Address: **Travel Program**
1865 Broadway
New York NY 10023
Phone: **(212)582-7500**
Fax: **(212)664-7653**
Contact: **Shirley Bakal, Director**

The Guild's annual tour of Eastern Europe includes a Gala New Year's Eve ball in Vienna's Palais Schwarzenberg, as well as visits Warsaw, Cracow, Prague and Budapest. The schedule is filled with performances of operas, concerts and recitals in magnificent refurbished theatres and historic concert halls. There are visits to Chopin's birthplace, Mozart's home, and outstanding cathedrals, palaces, and museums. Guild travelers stay in deluxe hotels and eat in some of the world's finest restaurants.

A Russian tour visits Moscow, Kiev, Odessa, Leningrad, and Helsinki where travelers attend opera, ballet, and concert performances.

You can join the Metropolitan Opera Guild for $40 a year, and be eligible for these tours and their trips to Spain, Morocco, Portugal, Paris, Strasbourg, Munich, Istanbul, Athens, and Naples. The majority of Guild tours take members overseas, but there are also special New York weekend programs with performances and musical events.

Price includes:

Accommodations in deluxe hotels, the best available tickets for performances, most meals, transportation, guides, lectures.

Sample trips:

$1,600 for three-day New York City Weekends.
$3,245 for two weeks in Russia (airfare included).
$5,725 for two weeks in Eastern Europe.

METROPOLITAN STATE COLLEGE

Address: Language and Culture Institute
Box 26
1006 11th Street
Denver CO 80204
Phone: (303)556-2908
Contact: Dr. David Conde

The Language and Culture Institute offers summer programs in France, Germany, and Spain for four weeks. Students must have one year of previous study in the language at college level.

In France, students attend the French American Study Center in Lisieux, on the Normandy coast. They live in an 18th century mansion next to the Center and attend classes five days a week, with excursions to cultural and historic sites on the other days.

In West Germany, students stay in modern, private rooms on the international campus of the Akadamie Klausenhof, in Hamminkeln. There are three weeks of intensive language classes six hours a day for six days a week, and a week of touring in the Alpine region of Bavaria.

In Spain, students attend two weeks of intensive language courses at the University of Navarra in Pamplona, and live at the Colegio Mayor of Pamplona. The third week is spent in cultural studies at the Colegio Lecaroz and the last week in Madrid visiting cultural and historic sites.

MSC also offers a two week tour of the Yucatan Peninsula in Mexico between the fall and spring semesters. The itinerary includes visits to Villahermosa, Palenque, Merida, Uxmal, Chichen Itza, and Cancun.

Price includes:

Accommodations, all meals, tuition, materials, entry fees, activities.

Sample trips:

$1,520 for four weeks in Germany.
$1,625 for four weeks in Spain.
$1,926 for four weeks in France.

MONTANA STATE UNIVERSITY

Address: **Adult Chamber Music Festival**
Music Department
Montana State University
Bozeman, MT 59717-0008
Phone: **(406)587-8220**
Messages: **(406)994-3561**
Contact: **Mary C. Sanks.**

The fresh, clear air of the Rocky Mountains surrounds musicians when they attend the week-long Adult Chamber Music Festival held every summer since 1971 on the campus of Montana State University. Designed for intermediate and advanced chamber music players, there are daily music assignments, music-sharing forums, master classes, demonstrations, orchestras, and time to browse through MSU's music library as well as playing for fun.

"We welcome any player of strings, wind instruments or piano at intermediate level or better, amateurs or professionals" notes Mary Sanks, the director. Players often bring their families who enjoy the Sunday family picnic supper, hiking, fishing, sketching, and the Museum of the Rockies, which offers social activities and even field trips to dig dinosaur eggs.

The campus is close to Yellowstone National Park and the Grand Tetons. Participants live in campus dorms.

Price includes:

Accommodations, meals, facilities, activities, tuition.

Sample Costs:

$165 for registration.
$400 for room and board.

MOUNTAIN TRAVEL

Address: **6420 Fairmont Avenue**
El Cerrito CA 94530
Phone: **(415)527-8100/(800)227-2384**
Contact: **Travel Director**

Leo Le Bon established Mountain Travel in 1967, and since then has been actively leading, scouting, and exploring treks around the world since then. The company has introduced over 10,000 clients to the joys of adventure travel.

This year, it published a 104-page illustrated brochure to describe more than 100 trips. Every one is graded as Easy, Moderate or Strenuous. They include trekking, skiing, inn-to-inn hiking, safaris, mountaineering, rafting, kayaking, canoeing, and adventure cruises. Mountain Travel also organizes seminars in Wilderness Medicine for health professionals.

Le Bon explains: "We design our trips to be informal yet genuine explorations by small groups: travels that not only challenge, but also promote greater cultural awareness, the enjoyment of the outdoors, and the preservation of our planet's wildlife and wilderness."

Mountain Travel leaders are carefully chosen for their understanding of the areas and cultures visited and their expertise as guides, naturalists, and mountaineers.

Tours include year-round adventures in Africa, Asia, South America, Europe, and North America. African safaris explore Kenya, Tanzania, Botswana, and the Sahara desert.

You can visit Antarctica and the Falkland Islands to see penguins, petrels, ancient volcanic calderas (craters), and seals basking on ice floes. In Asia there are treks to Mt. Everest, Kanchenjunga and Annapurna, among the highest mountains in the world. There's trekking in China and Pakistan and an elephant safari into the hills of Northern Thailand.

In South America you can tour Peru, Bolivia, Patagonia, Chile, and the ancient carved stone figures on Easter Island. European trips include inn-to-inn hiking in Switzerland, France, Italy, Germany, Spain, and Scotland among others. Pacific tours visit Australia's Great Barrier Reef, Indonesia, Bali, Borneo, New Guinea, and Hawaii.

Price includes:

Accommodationa, preparation materials, reading lists, trek and safari arrangements, most meals, airport transfers, transportation, leadership, guides, porters, equipment, entry fees, permits.

Sample trips:

(with fewer than 10 participants)

$830 for eight days, inn-to-inn hiking in Austria.
$1,395 for 13 days, Andean Lakes Overland, Chile.
$2,590 for 30 days, Ultimate Everest Trek.
$3,050 for 14 days, Tanzania Wildlife Safari.

"A first rate trip," noted a participant on the Tanzania Wildlife Safari. "The roar of lions on both sides of the tent at Kaabi Hill at night, watching them with their prey in the morning within a half mile of the tents is an unforgettable experience."

NANTAHALA OUTDOOR CENTER

Address: **US 19 W**
Box 41
Bryson City, NC 28713
Phone: **(704)488-2175**
Contact: **Janet Smith, Adventure Travel Coordinator**

Nantahala Outdoor Center is located in North Carolina near the heart of the Great Smoky Mountains, about 90 minutes' drive from Asheville, North Carolina and two hours from Chattanooga, Tennessee. Nearby is some of the best white water paddling, backpacking, climbing, biking, and fly fishing in the Southeast. Since 1972, NOC has been organizing trips to take advantage of these amenities.

You can go overnight backpacking and learn how to hike with a map and compass and to identify animal tracks. Or choose to spend a weekend learning the art of fly fishing, how to build a log cabin, or how to take great nature photographs.

The Center offers instruction programs on running white water in kayaks and canoes, workshops in Advanced Racing down rivers, training for river raft leadership and courses in emergency medical skills. There's plenty of wild river water for rafting—on the Nantahala, the French Broad, the Chatooga, the Ocoee, the Nolichucky, and the Chatooga for a more challenging experience. Part of the Chatooga, designated a National Wild and Scenic River, was the location for the movie *Deliverance.*

NOC trips abroad include kayaking in Scotland, rafting and kayaking on Mexico's Usumacinta River, in Costa Rica, in Chile, in Nepal, and in New Zealand. They also offer canoe and kayak trips in Alaska.

Price includes:

Accommodations, all meals, transportation, fees, equipment or rentals available.

Sample trips:

$320 for three days rock climbing in the Appalachians.
$410 for six-day hike and raft trip on Chattooga river.
$995 for 10-day raft and kayak trip in Costa Rica.
$2,300 for four weeks raft and kayak trip in Nepal.

NATIONAL AUDUBON SOCIETY

Address: 950 Third Avenue
New York NY 10022
Phone: (212)546-9140
Fax: (212)593-6254
Contact: Margaret Mullaly, Travel Manager

The National Audubon Society tours focus on birds, plants, animals, wildlife sanctuaries, and nature refuges. The Society has sponsored travel programs since the 1940s, and all tours are led by staff experts. Membership, $30 a year, is open to all.

Most Audubon trips are cruises, and the itineraries include Antarctica, South America, Baja California, and Greece as well as England, Venezuela, Belize, Kenya, and the Yucatan in Mexico. New trips for 1990 include a cruise around Indonesia, an exploration of Alaska's coastal wilderness by boat, a Costa Rica bicycling tour, and cruises to the Galapagos Islands.

In 1989, a growing concern for the environment led the Society to prepare "The National Audubon Society Travel Ethic for Environmentally Responsible travel."

This document demands adherence to high standards of environmental protection from all tour operators, leaders, and participants, who must agree to abide by its rules.

The key points emphasize that:

1. Wildlife and their habitats must not be disturbed.
2. Audubon tourism to natural areas will be sustainable.
3. Waste disposal must have neither environmental nor aesthetic impact.
4. The experience a tourist gains in traveling with Audubon must enrich his or her appreciation of nature, conservation, and the environment.
5. Audubon tours must strengthen the conservation effort and enhance the natural integrity of places visited.
6. Traffic in products that threaten wildlife and plant populations must not occur.
7. The sensibilities of other cultures must be respected.

"Our repeat travelers are growing every year" notes Margaret Mullaly, "and more and more of our passengers are traveling with Audubon for a second and third time."

Price includes:

Accommodations, all meals, excursions, lectures, guides.

Sample trips:

$1,890 for eight days/lower deck, Baja California.
$3,495 for 13 days/inside cabin, Istanbul, Aegean Sea.
$6,975 for 20 days/yacht deck, South American coast.
$15,345 for 21 days/suite, Antarctica, Falkland Islands.

NATIONAL OUTDOOR LEADERSHIP SCHOOL

Address: Box AA
Lander WY 82520
Phone: (307)332-6973
Fax: (307)332-3631
Contact: Sukey Richard

Want to learn to climb mountains, backpack, kayak, and trek through wilderness? The National Outdoor Leadership School, founded in 1965 by Paul Petzoldt, has introduced over 25,000 people to environmentally sound outdoor camping, hiking, climbing, and boating through its courses in the Rocky Mountains, Pacific Northwest, Alaska, Mexico, South America, and Africa.

"We teach people how to *not* get into a survival situation and how comfortable it can be to live in the outdoors," explained Jim Ratz, Executive Director. "NOLS is a place to learn about caring for the land. Our courses are rigorous, but the pace is designed to allow everyone to keep up and build upon what they have learned each day."

The NOLS Core Curriculum covers safety and judgment, leadership and expedition dynamics, minimum-impact camping and resource protection, environmental awareness, outdoor living skills, travel techniques, and public services issues. Courses run for a three-month semester, or for two, three or four weeks. Students range in age from 14 to 75, although the majority are college students in their twenties. There are special summer courses designed for people aged 25 and over.

Semester courses explore specific regions: Kenya, Wyoming, Alaska, New Mexico and the Southwest, and Patagonia at the tip of Chile and Argentina. Participants learn a variety of skills, depending on the terrain—backpacking, horsepacking, white water rafting, fishing, kayaking, caving, hiking, and rock climbing. They also learn food preparation and minimum-impact camping.

Price includes:

Accommodations, field rations, instruction, equipment, transportation. Some scholarships and financial aid are available.

Sample trips:

$1,550 for four-week Outdoor Educators Course, Washington
$2,100 for four-week Wilderness Course, Wyoming.
$4,500 for three-month semester, Arizona and the Southwest.
$5,700 for three-month semester, Kenya.

One participant said: "It is not only a great experience learning rock climbing, kayaking or backcountry skills, but it is also a springboard from which you can develop and test your own ideas on personal stewardship of the earth."

NATIONAL REGISTRATION CENTER FOR STUDY ABROAD

Address: **823 North 2nd Street**
Milwaukee WI 53203
Phone: **(414)278-0631**
Contact: **Mike Wittig**

The NRCSA is a consortium of 86 schools and adult education centers in 16 countries. In 1988, NRCSA members reported that over 12,000 Americans traveled and studied with them, ranging in age from 16 to 84. One survey showed that in some regions, such as Mexico and Costa Rica, there are more younger students in the summer, and more mature adults in the late fall, winter, and spring.

Over 3,000 courses a year are available through NRCSA's

foreign centers which offer courses on learning a second language in a foreign country as well as scores of others on the arts, architecture, literature, and more. Students sign up for a week, a month, or several months.

NRSCA offers tours for teenagers, who generally travel in groups accompanied by a home schoolteacher. Teen programs include trips to Mexico, Spain, Austria, Germany, Italy, and Switzerland.

For adults, NRSCA arrange Center Programs with visits to London and Paris, with excursions for pub lunches and traditional cuisine; a trip to Quito, Ecuador with Spanish language classes and cultural tours for a week, followed by an Amazon cruise; or studying German, Italian or French in Austria for 2 weeks followed by two weeks touring Germany, Italy and Switzerland to practice new language skills.

The NRSCA also publishes course catalogs listing university/adult courses in Britain, canal cruising, cycling and walking in Britain, places to study Spanish in Central and South America, French in France & Switzerland, and Italian in Italy, among others.

Membership is $30 a year. Members receive all catalogs plus a three-year subscription to *New Horizons*, the semi-annual newsletter of updated information. Send a self-addressed business envelope with 45 cents postage to receive the most recent newsletter.

Price includes:

Accommodations, all meals, lectures, field trips.

Sample trips:

$537 for two weeks of Italian in Rome, Italy.
$1,265 for two weeks in Britain and France.
$1,975 for five weeks of French in Switzerland.
$4,407 for 13 weeks of German in Koln, Germany.

NATIONAL WILDLIFE FEDERATION

Address: **1400 16th Street NW**
Washington, DC 20036-2266
Phone: **(703)790-4363**
Contact: **Steve Law**

The National Wildlife Federation is the world's largest and most influential organization of private citizens promoting the wise use of natural resources. The Federation is composed of affiliate organizations in nearly every state and territory, and also has Associate Members around the country.

NWF publishes *National Wildlife,* and *International Wildlife* magazines for adults and families, and *Ranger Rick* and *Your Big Backyard* for children. The NWF science and social studies curriculum for middle schools is distributed through its workshop system, and it also distributes millions of Wildlife Conservation Stamps each year.

Its educational programs include award-winning Wildlife Camps for children in Colorado and North Carolina, Teen Adventure Programs for young people aged 13-17, workshops and special training for local conservation leaders, and outdoor discovery vacations, called Conservation Summits, for adults and families.

The Summit programs, organized in the summer in Colorado, North Carolina, Vermont, and Washington, allow adults and families to design their own schedules, choosing from about 20 different classes and field trips on ecology, bird watching, nature photography, geology, and more, depending on the region. In the evening, there are square dances, slide shows, sing-alongs, and other cultural events.

There are special Summits for educators in Black Mountain, North Carolina.

Price includes:

Accommodations, all meals, recreational facilities, excursions. NWF Membership fee: $15 a year.

Sample Costs:

Study Program fees: $200 per adult per week/$140 for children/$70 for preschoolers.
Room and board fees: $200 a week for adult sharing room for four, Colorado.
$331 a week for adult, single room, Vermont.

"The new information I've gained about ecology is fantastic!" noted an educator. "I will use it at school as well as at home."

NATURE EXPEDITIONS INTERNATIONAL

Address: **PO Box 11496**
Eugene, OR 97440
Phone: **(503)484-6529/(800)869-0639**
Contact: **David Roderick, President**

Wildlife and natural history expeditions in Alaska, Hawaii, the Andes, Mexico, Africa, Bhutan, the Himalayas, Nepal, Australia, New Zealand, and Papua New Guinea are the specialty of Nature Expeditions International.

Some 90 trips are offered year-round. They include a safari to East Africa; exploring the ancient Mayan civilization of Mexico; touring in Australian national parks; and walks along New Zealand's famous treks in February and March, when it's summer there.

"Our concept of combining learning on vacation with adventure and discovery allows everyone to be a modern explorer of planet Earth," declares David Roderick, who started the company in 1973. "It's the only way we can really understand

Most of the men and women who participate are "inquisitive, enthusiastic people who share an interest in natural history, photography, and anthropology," and range in age from 25 to 75.

Every NEI leader is well-qualified with experience in the host country and has an M.A. or Ph.D. degree or equivalent professional training, and teaching experience at college level. NEI has also arranged trips for groups, including the New York Zoological Society, California Academy of Sciences, and the Stanford Alumni Association.

Price includes:

Accommodations, most meals, land/sea transportation, transfers, entrance fees, service charges, tips, instruction, leadership.

Sample trips:

$1,790 for 16 days in Mexico and Yucatan.
$2,190 for 15 days in Hawaii.
$3,990 for 23 days in the Himalayas.
$4,590 for 25 days in East Africa and Rwanda.

One science editor who went on the East Africa Wildlife Safari commented: "Most exciting thing I've done in my life. Sitting among gorillas was like having dinner with eccentric relatives. You don't know what to say to them, but it's so nice to see them and just sit around and visit."

NEWARK MUSEUM

Address: **49 Washington Street**
Box 540
Newark NJ 07101
Phone: **(201)596-6550**
Fax: **(201)642-0459**
Contact: **Barbara Lowell, Director, Membership/Museum Services**

Art-related trips are organized by the newly expanded and renovated Newark Museum. The Museum has an extensive collection of 19th and 20th century American art and is ranked among the top 10 museums in the country for its American paintings. On display are Hudson River School landscapes by Thomas Cole, Asher B. Durant, and Jasper Cropsey, as well as American Impressionists, and still life paintings and portraits by such artists as Edward Hopper, Max Weber, John Sloan, and Georgia O'Keeffe.

The Museum offers members and guests weekend trips, including a visit to Washington, DC to see exhibitions at the National Gallery of Art; to Sante Fe, New Mexico to observe local artists' work; and to Pennsylvania to tour "Fallingwater," one of the houses designed by architect Frank Lloyd Wright, and art exhibitions.

Abroad, members have traveled to Turkey and the ancient cities of Aphrodisias, Miletus, Ephesus, and Troy; to the Russian Winter Arts Festival in Leningrad and Moscow; and to Brazil tracing the development of Brazilian art and culture from colonial to modern times.

The Museum also organizes a bus service to take members to special exhibitions at New York City's Metropolitan Museum of Art and Museum of Modern Art.

Price includes:

Accommodations, transportation, all meals, lectures and admissions.

Sample trips:

$350 for weekend in Washington, DC.
$1,050 for a week in Santa Fe, NM.
$2,400 for 14 days in France.

NEW YORK BOTANICAL GARDEN

Address: **200th Street and Southern Blvd**
Bronx NY 10458-5126
Phone: **(212)220-8700**
Fax: **(212)220-6504**
Contact: **Carol Gracie, Travel Program Director**

The New York Botanical Garden offers several trips to its members. A group of eight volunteers can join a research expedition in French Guiana led by Dr. Scott Mori and his wife, Carol Gracie, to collect and process plants, observe pollination, and assist with forest ecology studies.

"Volunteers need not have a background in botany," note the leaders, "but they must be physically fit, willing to live and work in less than ideal conditions, and enthusiastic team workers."

There's also a 10-day Ethnobotanical Research Expedition to Belize in Central America, led by Dr. Michael Balick. His project involves working with Belize herbalists to learn which plants are used locally for medicinal purposes. Participants will have time to visit archeological sites nearby,as well as the offshore islands of Belize's barrier reef.

For less active travelers, there is a cruise around the Galapagos Islands of Ecuador to observe its unique flora and fauna and a cruise down the Amazon, led by a Brazilian naturalist, to learn about the rich plant and animal life of the rain forest. Garden lovers can choose to cruise around Great Britain to see estates in Cornwall, Wales, and Scotland with dazzling flowers in herbaceous borders, rock gardens, formal parks, and indoor conservatories.

Price includes:

Airfare, accommodations, most meals, activities, guides. Add a $300 donation to NYBG.

Sample trips:

$1,975 for 10 days research expedition in Belize.
$2,795 for two-week cruise down Amazon in Brazil.
$3,495 for 16 days in Galapagos (from Miami).
$6,900 for two-week cruise to British gardens.

NORTH CAROLINA CENTRAL UNIVERSITY

Address: **Summer Study in France**
Dept. of Modern Foreign Languages
214 Communications Building
Durham, NC 27707
Phone: **(919)560-6331**
Contact: **Rebekah B. Wade, Program Coordinator**

The university arranges summer sessions of French-language studies in the south of France, at the Centre International d'Etudes Francaise of the University of Nice. Classes are geared to all levels, and there are also seminars on French literature, civilization, and business. The session includes some touring and a week in Paris.

Participants are usually students from North Carolina Central University and teachers from the public schools, but the sessions are open to any interested adult.

"In Nice, the courses are intensive and the excursions to places of interest are numerous," notes Rebekah Wade. "In Paris, there are visits to the major monuments and museums and optional day trips to Versailles and Chartres."

Price includes:

Airfare, accommodations, most meals, transportation, insurance, tuition.

Sample trips:

$2,500 for four weekw for North Carolina students.
$3,500 for four weeks for out-of-state students.

NORTH CASCADES INSTITUTE

Address: **2105 Highway 20**
Sedro Woolley, WA 98284
Phone: **(206)856-5700**
Contact: **Robyn du Pre, Admin. Assistant**

Outdoor seminars that take participants into the beautiful scenery of the region are the specialty of North Cascades Institute.

Participants hike to Swakane Canyon to observe butterflies in the North Cascades; backpack to the Pasayten Wilderness to read poetry and prose amid the mountains; and hike to the Lake Chelan-Sawtooth Wilderness Area to look for wildflowers.

"We strive for small, informal classes, bringing together interested and eager learners. Our instructors are expert teachers who take delight in sharing their expertise," notes Saul Weisberg, Executive Director. "We seek to increase understanding and appreciation of the natural, historical and cultural legacy of the North Cascades."

Founded in 1985, the Institute offers some 80 courses related to the North Cascade Mountains of Washington State. They include nature writing, art, and photography as well as seminars on raptors, rocks, minerals and fossils, marine mammals, meteorology, amphibians, and birds. The Institute runs from January through October and all classes take place in the mountains, forests, and river valleys and along the shoreline of the region.

Price includes:

Course fee only. Participants are responsible for their own food and transportation. Most seminars are held in National Park or Forest Service campgrounds.

Sample Courses:

$75 for two days on Northwest Mushrooms.
$90 for three days, Wilderness Education Workshop.
$125 for three days, Butterflies of the North Cascades.

O.A.R.S. INC.

Address: **PO Box 67**
Angels Camp CA 95722
Phone: **(209)736-4677**
Fax: **(209)736-2902**
Contact: **Kay Metherell**

"When my wife and I first established O.A.R.S. 17 years ago, we were doing river trips for fun because we wanted to do them," notes George Wendt, president of the company. "Now, I've found that I need a river trip just to clean the clutter from my mind and to revitalize my soul."

O.A.R.S. stands for Outdoor Adventure River Specialists, and the company runs Western river trips throughout the summer with qualified guides who know a great deal about the regions they raft through. You travel in inflatable kayaks, oar or paddle boats, or wooden dories, and trips last from a day to a couple of weeks. The company rents out a video on river rafting to show what it's like.

There are trips down the Colorado through the Grand Canyon, on the San Juan and Dolores Rivers in Utah; through Cataract Canyon, known for its wild rapids; and on the Yampa River in Utah. Boats raft through Desolation and Gray Canyons on the Green River; on the Rogue River in Oregon; and on the American, Kern, Klamath, Tuolumne, Merced and Stanislaus in California; and down the Salmon and Selway in Idaho.

Price includes:

Accommodations camping, all meals, river equipment, transportation to and from meeting place. Camping equipment rentals available.

Sample trips:

$84 for day trip on American North Fork, California.
$490 for four days on Rogue River in Oregon.
$665 for six days, Desolation/Gray Canyons in dories.
$1,955 for 13 days through Grand Canyon.

"Even those that think they are weak at heart will have much more confidence and self-reliance at the end, to say nothing of the awesome scenery they will take in," a woman from North Carolina wrote after her rafting trip.

OFFSHORE SAILING SCHOOL

Address: **16731-110 McGregor Boulevard**
Fort Myers FL 33908
Phone: **(800)221-4326**
Fax; **(813)454-1191**
Contact: **Kirk Williams**

Steve Colgate, who learned to sail at the age of nine and is an America's Cup and Olympic sailor, promises students that after taking his course, they will know how to sail. Today, more than 60,000 people have earned the Offshore diploma.

Steve started teaching in 1964 with one boat and one instructor. Now he and his wife Doris, who met him when she took his class, supervise sailing schools in Captiva Island, Florida; on two Caribbean islands; and at Chatham, Cape Cod. There's also a school on City Island, in New York City.

The basic Learn to Sail courses start every week on Sunday. Beginners use an Olympic Class 27 foot Soling, with four students per instructor. They learn nautical terminology, rigging and sails, getting under way, proper winching techniques, tacking and jibing, sailing backward, knots, steering with a compass, navigation and more.

Colgate's Basic Sailing Theory is the textbook ,and Offshore School instructors follow the time-tested curriculum carefully, plus hours and hours of hands-on sailing.

ZThere are also classes in Advanced Sailing, Introductory and Advanced Racing, and Bareboat Cruising Preparation as well as a Live Aboard Cruising course.

Price includes:

Accommodations, tuition, meals, party, textbook, certificate, wallet card, logbook. Airfare, hotel tax, service charges not included.

Sample trips:

$847 for six days in Florida, July to December.
$1,254 for eight days in Florida, January and February.
$1,180 for eight days in the Caribbean, Nov/December.

A doctor from Minnesota noted: "Learning to sail was the fulfillment of a lifelong dream The course was intense, well taught, and achieved the desired reults. It was invigorating and reassuring that one can learn a new skill well after age 50, and disproved the adage that you can't teach an old dog new tricks!"

OUR DEVELOPING WORLD

Address: **13004 Paseo Presada**
Saratoga CA 95070
Phone: **(408)376-0755**
Contact: **Vic and Barby Ulmer**

The organization's aim is to bring the realities of the Third World to North Americans through programs in schools, churches, and community groups. They also arrange study tours to the Philippines, Cuba, Hawaii, Mozambique, Zimbabwe, Honduras, and Nicaragua which focus on social, economic, and political issues.

"Our study tours emphasize people and development," notes a staff member. "We firmly believe in responsible tourism."

In Hawaii, participants examine efforts to preserve Hawaiian indigenous culture against the impact of militarism, tourism, and commercial development. Talks with Hawaiian leaders and the U.S. military are included.

In Mozambique and Zimbabwe, the program compares and contrasts the two recently independent neighbors. And in the Philippines, Honduras, and Nicaragua, participants examine human rights and the effect of land reform; visit farms and factories; and meet social workers, tribal peoples, educators, health workers, and government officials.

Price includes:

Airfare (from San Francisco), accommodations, most meals, transportation, transfers, guides, translators, facilitators.

Sample trips:

$869 for a week in Hawaii.
$1,459 for two weeks in Honduras and Nicaragua.
$1,895 for two weeks in the Philippines.
$3,695 for three weeks in Mozambique/Zimbabwe from New York.

OUTWARD BOUND USA

Address: 384 Field Point Road
Greenwich CT 06830
Phone: (203)661-0797/(800)243-8520
Fax: (203)661-0903
Contact: Director

Outward Bound is the largest and oldest adventure-based education organization in the United States. Its wilderness programs operate through five schools in Colorado, Maine, Minnesota, North Carolina, and Oregon. Over 190,000 people have participated in these courses in 22 states.

The programs are designed to challenge the participant's spirit, initiative, and ability to work with others while achieving common goals. The courses usually have no more than 12 people and teach technical skills for wilderness survival. There are also professional development programs for corporations, a Youth-at-Risk program, and semester-long programs for college students and educators.

The Kurt Hahn Leadership School offers leadership training in rock climbing, mountain rescue, and wilderness emergency medical care. City programs operate in some urban areas, including New York, Los Angeles, and Chicago.

The people who take Outward Bound courses come from all walks of life—college students, high-school students, business executives, writers, parents, grandparents, teachers, factory workers—and can be any age. Most of them have little or no experience in the wilderness but are in reasonably good shape.

Bill Abelow, a trustee of North Carolina Outward Bound School, describes Outward Bound's goals as, "Accomplishing things you never in a million years thought you could even try and recognizing that, although you have limits, they are nowhere near what you thought,"

Price includes:

Accommodations, meals, tuition, equipment (not footwear). Financial aid is given to about 25 percent of students.

Sample trips:

$850 for six days horse-trailing in Utah.
$1,275 for 15 days backpacking in Montana.
$2,000 for 21 days climbing and trekking in Tanzania.

"I have pushed, stretched, pulled and twisted myself to go beyond my so called limits. Now I can do things I want to do and know that failure isn't so bad, but to not try is worse," noted a 45 year old participant in an Outward Bound course.

OVERSEAS ADVENTURE TRAVEL

Address: 349 Broadway
Cambridge MA 02139
Phone: (617)876-0533/(800)221-0814
Fax: (617)876-0455
Contact: Judi Wineland, President

Since 1979, Overseas Adventure Travel has offered adventure travel to Africa, Asia, South America and Pacific Rim countries; some trips are designed to include children.

The leaders are expert staff members who often live in the regions that are visited and know the local customs and procedures.

OAT is the only travel company endorsed by the African Wildlife Foundation, because of its strong commitment to conservation.

"We are scrupulous in our camp sanitation, cook only with liquid fuel in deforested areas, and have pioneered innovative techniques of trash and solid waste disposal," a staff member points out.

In Africa, OAT leads safaris to Tanzania's Rift Valley, Maasailand, the Ngorongoro Crater with its thousands of pink flamingoes, and Serengeti Park. Another safari explores the Virunga Mountains, the habitat of the mountain gorillas. And there's a special trip to watch the migration of the wildebeests, zebras and gazelles across the Serengeti.

Other trips travel to Morocco's Atlas Mountains and the towns of Fez, Marrakech, and Casablanca. In Egypt, there's a journey on the Nile aboard a traditional 'felucca' sailboat, with stops at ancient temples and pyramids. In the Himalayas, there are trekking, rafting, and wildlife expeditions to see Kathmandu, Everest, Annapurna, Tibet, and Leh. The South American trips visit the Andes, Macchu Picchu, the Amazon jungle, Ecuador, the Galapagos Islands, and the wonders of Patagonia. In Java and Bali, travelers discover the beauties of the festivals, music, art, and dance of the region.

Price includes:

Accommodations, all meals, transportation, guides, excursions, fees. Airfare not included although OAT can book group rates.

Sample trips:

$1,630 for two weeks on the Nile.
$2,200 for three weeks in Java and Bali.
$2,420 for two weeks in Africa.

"You made my dream come true," wrote a participant. "To see Tanzania wildlife and the Serengeti in all its splendor. I am still riding high on a cloud from my trip. It was wonderful. For my first time camping, it was so easy."

PACIFIC EXPLORATION COMPANY

Address: Box 3042
Santa Barbara, CA 93130
Phone: (805)687-7282
Fax: (805)569-0722
Contact: Ronald Richardson, Director

"We custom-design independent tour itineraries for individuals, families, and small groups who want a travel program which allows them to experience the beauty and excitement of the natural environment," explains Ronald Richardson. The trips focus on nature, hiking, and the outdoors in the South Pacific region.

The company, founded in 1976, sends travelers a questionnaire about where and when they like to travel, the kind of places in which they prefer to stay, and the activities which most interest them and outlines of trips are enclosed as a guide.

A four week tour of New Zealand, for example, includes a safari in Urewara National Park with Maori guides; a hike across the steaming volcanic floor in Tongariro National Park; a five day walk along the Milford Track through the unspoiled Southern Alps wilderness of Fjordland National Park;and visits to a working sheep station, the glow-worm caves of Waitomo, the hot springs of Rotorua, and the cities of Christchurch, Queenstown, and Auckland.

In Australia, travelers can take a horse trek in the Snowy Mountains; a hiking and camping tour of Kakadu National Park; a camping safari from Alice Springs into the vast Central Desert; and a week's sailing on the Great Barrier Reef.

Participants can stop over en route in the Polynesian islands of Fiji, Tahiti, and Rarotonga on the flight home.

Price includes:

Accommodations, all meals, transportation, guides.

Sample trips:

$1,975 for 18-day Australia tour.
$2,490 for 22-day New Zealand Walkabout.
$2,400 for 24 days of sea kayaking, Great Barrier Reef, Australia.

PACIFIC NORTHWEST FIELD SEMINARS

Address: 83 South King Street, Suite 212
Seattle WA 98104
Phone: (206)442-2636
Fax: (206)442-4896
Contact: R. Alan Mebane, Field Seminar Coordinator

A series of outdoor seminars are held every summer in the national parks and forests of Washington and Oregon. Topics covered include natural history, wildlife, astronomy, painting, outdoor writing, history, and photography taught by experts in the field.

There's a two day course on painting at Mount Rainier, led by a regional landscape painter, and courses on sketching, nature writing, and listening. There are introductory courses on astronomy as well as family camping trips and backpacking for women Other seminars focus on birds, on alpine ecology and ancient forests, on the Indians and settlers of Oregon, the geology of Mount Hood, and the coastal environment. Some seminars are designed for the handicapped.

Ever since the eruption of Mount St. Helens in 1980, there has been great interest in the volcano and the changes resulting from the eruption. One seminar, led by volcanologist Chris Jonientz-Trisler, takes a group on a 12-mile hike around the eruption area. Others examine the geology, the wildlife, and the glaciology of the volcano.

Price includes:

Tuition only. Accommodations and meals available locally but participants make their own arrangements.

Sample courses:

$30 for one day, Night Skies of the Northwest.
$60 for two days, Hiking through volcanic Landscapes.
$90 for two days, Nature Writing at Mount Rainier.

PARSONS SCHOOL OF DESIGN

Address: **Summer Programs**
66 Fifth Avenue
New York, NY 10011
Phone: **(212)741-8975**
Contact: **Francine Goldenhar, Director of Special Programs**

Parsons School of Design, founded in 1896, is one of the most comprehensive colleges of the visual arts in the United States. It strives to create opportunities for cross-cultural exchange while providing rigorous training in the full range of the design professions and the fine arts.

Every summer, intensive study programs in France, Italy, England, West Africa, Israel, and Japan are offered to students, graduates, teachers, designers, and artists. In Paris, a study of European art and architecture is conducted in collaboration with the Musee des Arts Decoratifs. There is also a special program on photography, with access to a darkroom. Class assignments emphasize composition and printing skills.

In Japan, participants meet internationally recognized Japanese designers in advertising, publishing, typography, and packaging through lectures, field trips, and visits to museums, galleries, and studios.

The program in Israel focuses on drawing, painting, and archaeology, with visits to Christian, Jewish and Moslem sites of significance. And in West Africa, participants explore the traditional African arts of ceramics, fiber arts, metalsmithing, and building in villages in the Ivory Coast and Mali.

Price includes:

Airfare, accommodations, some meals, transportation, tuition, college credits.

Sample trips:

$3,095 for a month of photography in Paris.
$3,640 for a month in Israel.
$5,160 for a month in Japan.

PEOPLE TO PEOPLE INTERNATIONAL

Address: **501 East Armour Boulevard**
Kansas City, MO 64109
Phone: **(816)531-4701**
Fax: **(816)561-6502**
Contact: **Alan M. Warne, V.P., Programs**

People to People International was created by President Dwight Eisenhower in 1956 to further world peace and understanding through exchanges between private citizens. There are more than 150 chapters in 34 countries around the world. The organization offers Travel Study, Pen Pal, Magazine Exchange and High School Student Ambassador programs.

Co-sponsored by the University of Missouri-Kansas City, PPI summer traveling seminars focus on specific topics In Stockholm, it's issues in special education, and an examination of man in relation to his environment.

In Washington, DC the emphasis is on Europe; an international business seminar takes participants first to meetings with government officials followed by a tour of London, Holland, Belgium and France to learn about the background and present situation of European business. It is led by Dr. Fred Hays, professor of banking, University of Missouri-Kansas City.

There is also an eight week internship program in England and Ireland where students work unpaid for a company or public organization to gain work experience abroad. The programs may be combined with a 12 day tour of Holland, Germany, Belgium and France.

A travel program in Costa Rica, led by professional naturalists, explores the neotropical biology of the region in the Monteverde Cloud Forest Reserve, the Carara Biological Reserve and the Manual Antonio National Park, among others. A Mexican program follows the 1519 route Cortez and his soldiers and visits the historic cities of Cempoala, Xalapa, Tlaxcala, Cholula, and Mexico City. Special guest classes will be held at the University of Mexico and Vera Cruz-Xalapa.

Price includes:

Airfare, accommodations in hotels or dorms, some meals, tuition, educational materials, transportation, entrance fees, excursions.

Sample trips:

$975 for 12-day "Discover Europe" (no airfare).
$2,175 for 16 days in Mexico.
$2,375 for 13 days in Costa Rica.
$3,675 for four-week program, International Business.

PRATT INSTITUTE

Address: School of Continuing Education
200 Willoughby Avenue
Brooklyn, NY 11205
Phone: (718)636-3453
Fax: (718)622-6174
Contact: Judith Aaron, Dean

The Pratt Institute specializes in art, design, illustration, and computer graphics. Its faculty are mostly working professionals in the field, who carefully design courses geared to the realities of the marketplace.

The School of Continuing Education sponsors a variety of travel study programs for students, or professional illustrators, designers, architects, and artists. Each program combines architecture or art and design with travel.

One program offers six weeks in Venice studying at the Universita Internazionale dell'Arte in the Pallazzo Fortuny. Painting, drawing, and art history classes are taught by Pratt faculty members.

A trip to Japan for its architecture and culture includes visits to Frank Lloyd Wright's hotel in Nagoya, to Japan's oldest temples and largest Buddha in Nara, and to Tokyo's National Gymnasium, as well as to homes and professional offices of Japanese architects.

The long-established summer program in Copenhagen, Denmark, offers a three-month study course on architecture and design. Classes are taught in English by professors from the University of Copenhagen. The programs also tours much of Denmark, with trips to Stockholm, Sweden and Helsinki, Finland.

Price includes:

Airfare, accommodations, tuition, credits.

Sample trips:

$3,395 for two weeks in Japan (from California).
$3,850 for six week sin Venice (airfare not included).
$5,900 for summer in Denmark.

RAMAPO COLLEGE OF NEW JERSEY

Address: International Education
505 Ramapo Valley Road
Mahwah, NJ 07430-1680
Phone: (201)529-7463
Contact: Wayne C. Marshall, Office of International Education

Accredited summer study programs at the University of Bath, England, are offered by Ramapo College. Since 1983, hundreds of students from more than 60 colleges throughout the country have enrolled.

The five-week program is open to anyone with at least 30 college credits. Mature adults with a high school diploma may audit the courses. The 1990 courses of study include Economics of the European Economic Community, Europe Towards 1992, Modern British Drama, History of Bath and the West Country, Shakespeare as Social Commentator, and International Marketing.

Classes are conducted by British faculty and meet four mornings a week. There are also theater performances, a guided tour of Bath, and excursions to Stratford, Glastonbury, and Wells.

The optional six-week program includes a week in London and visits to Hampton Court Palace, Stonehenge, and Avebury.

The city of Bath is famous for its historic and literary heritage, its imposing Georgian architecture, and its Roman baths. Situated about an hour west of London, the city offers easy access to Wales, Scotland, Ireland, France, and Holland for weekend trips.

Price includes:

Airfare, accommodations, meal allowance, tuition, transportation, excursions, performances, activities.

Sample trips:

$1,995 for five weeks, Bath only.
$2,350 for six weeks, London and Bath.

READERS THEATER

Address: **International Summer Workshops**
PO Box 17193
San Diego, CA 92117
Phone: **(619)276-1048]**
Contact: **Dr. William Adams, Director**

Readers Theatre was founded in 1973 by Dr. Adams to encourage academic interest in group performance of literature and is a classroom strategy for effective teaching of any subject. The Institute publishes a Readers Theatre Script Service of scripts prepared for use in classrooms and gives workshops to educators around the country on the system.

The summer workshop in London organized by the Institute includes storytelling, creative dramatics, performance, scriptmaking, voice, and diction. There are lectures and seminars in the mornings, and the rest of the day and weekends are free. Students in speech, theatre and education, teachers, and "other adventurous people" may attend.

An entertainment package of visits to places of interest in London and day-trips to Cambridge, York, Bath, Canterbury, Brighton, Oxford, or Stratford is available at additional cost.

On alternate years, workshops are held in other locations. In the past these have included Hawaii, Vienna, Aix-en-Provence, Madrid, Vancouver, San Diego, and Athens.

Price includes:

Accommodations, breakfast, tuition, and fees.

Sample trip:

$1,575 for three weeks in London, July 8-27, 1990.

ROCKLAND COMMUNITY COLLEGE

Address: **State University of New York**
Center for International Studies
145 College Road
Suffern NY 10901
Phone: **(914)356-4650**
Fax: **(914)356-1529**
Contact: **Jody A. Dudderar**

Rockland Community College's Center for International Studies, which has served the college since 1968, offers study tours abroad to Rockland college students and those from other colleges, as well as to interested adults.

The most popular tour is Wintersession in London. The varied program of seminars and tours includes Broadcasting in Britain, which takes participants to watch studio tapings of programs at BBC-TV; at the commercial TV companies of Thames, London Weekend and Granada; and at ABC-TV's London office Another seminar focuses on criminal justice in Britain, with visits to the Old Bailey, the courts, and the prisons to hear lectures by experienced police, court and prison personnel.

Other seminar topics cover British history; an examination of English food and drink, with pub visits, a brewery tour, and tea at the Waldorf Hotel; and a look at nursing, real estate and international business

The college also offers study trips to Brussels, Cologne, Paris, Spain, and Morocco.

Price includes:

Airfare, accommodations, some meals, tuition, visits, lectures.

Sample trip:

$968 for two weeks of London Wintersession.

SAFARIWORLD!

Address: 40 East 49th Street
New York NY 10017
Phone: (212)486-0505/(800)366-0505
Fax: (212)486-0783
Contact: Jane Zalman

Safariworld! is one of the oldest safari companies in the United States and offers dozens of trips in Africa as well as several in Egypt, Mauritius, and the Seychelles Islands. The emphasis is on quality and elegance. Travelers stay in the Nairobi Safari Club, the Aberdare Country Club, and the Nguilia Safari Lodge, or enjoy comfortable bush camping. Game drives in safari vans guarantee window seats for all passengers, and there are also flights over some of the game preserves.

Guides and escorts are carefully chosen for their abilities and positive attitude and their extensive knowledge of the wildlife, native tribes, geography, and history of Africa.

In Kenya, travelers explore Masai Amboseli Game Reserve where hippos wallow at Mzima Springs and Mount Kilimanjaro rises to 19,340 feet crowned with white snow. The tour travels through Kikiyu country to the Sambura Game Reserve, on to Lake Naivasha, and across the Great Rift Valley to the Masai Mara Game Reserve where herds of elephants, giraffes and other animals roam freely.

Other tours travel to Tanzania and the Ngorongoro Crater in Serengeti National Park; to Rwanda and Zaire to see Akagera National Park, where leopards, lions, zebras, buffaloes, hippos and antelopes live undisturbed; and to the dense forest in Volcanoes National Park at Kinigi to look for mountain gorillas in their natural habitat. Private tented safaris can be arranged.

Price includes:

Accommodations, meals, transportation, guides, land arrangements. Prices vary according to season. Airfare not included but special Pan Am rates from New York to Nairobi are available.

Sample trips:

$1,799 to $2,199 for Safari Explorer, 14 days in Kenya.
$2,799 to $3,199 for Wings Over Mara, 15 days, Kenya.
$2,849 to $3,249 for 17 days in Kenya and Tanzania.

"We have traveled the world over and we would say that this trip was the best, the most outstanding one we have ever taken," commented a couple from San Francisco. "Due to the eagle-eyed guide, we saw almost every animal in Kenya."

SAINT ANSELM COLLEGE

Address: **87 Saint Anselm Drive**
Manchester NH 03102
Phone: **(603)641-7044**
Contact: **John D. Windhausen**

Since 1966, Saint Anselm's College has organized 18 annual trips to Russia for its students and other interested adults.

In June, the group flies from Boston to Helsinki and Leningrad, then travels for 14 days to Tbilisi, Yalta, Moscow, Talinin in Estonia, and back to Helsinki. There are visits to artistic and religious centers and the site of the famous Yalta Conference, tours of Russia's Hermitage and the Winter Palace, and an evening cruise to Finland. History Professors John Windhausen and Jack Lynch are the leaders.

Price includes:

Airfare, first class hotels, meals, guides, escorted tours, two theater tickets.

Sample trip:

$2,640 for three weeks in Russia.

SAINT MARY'S COLLEGE

Address: London & Rome Programs
Saint Mary's College
Notre Dame IN 46556-5001
Phone: (219)284-4460
Contact: Professor Anthony R. Black

A month in London followed by a month in Rome for students and interested adults are offered by Saint Mary's College. The London Program is in its 17th year, the Rome Program its 14th.

"A few alumnae and adults sign up, though most travelers are college students," notes Professor Black. Students come from Saint Mary's, Notre Dame University, and some thirty colleges and universities nationwide.

The London program begins with a week in Ireland and Scotland and then settles in London for seminars on British life. There are visits and tours to places of interest as well as excursions outside London.

The Rome program takes students first to Paris for a week, and then travels through Europe visiting Strasbourg, Lucerne, Venice, and Florence. In Rome, there are Italian-language classes as well as tours and visits to sites of interest.

Price includes:

Airfare, accommodations, some meals, transportation, tuition, excursions, guides. Add $100 airfare supplement for non-students or those over 26.

Sample trips:

$2,795 for one-month London Program.
$3,655 for one-month Rome Program.

SAN FRANCISCO STATE UNIVERSITY

Address: **European Studies Association**
City College of San Francisco
780 Monterey Blvd., Suite 203
San Francisco CA 94127
Phone: **(415)333-1040**
Fax: **(415)337-6030**
Contact: **Tom Blair**

Semester and summer study programs in Tokyo, Stratford-on-Avon, Florence, Heidelberg, Madrid, and Paris are open to all students through San Francisco State University's European Studies Association.

In Japan, participants live with a family in Tokyo, attend language and culture classes, and travel outside the city to Kyoto, Hiroshima, and Kamakura.

The Paris program provides French-language courses at the Sorbonne, and students live in dorms near the Luxembourg Gardens. There are visits to Mont St. Michel, St. Malo, Fontainebleau, Chartres Cathedral, Monet's home in Giverny, the Loire Valley, and Normandy.

In Florence, students live with Italian families, take classes in Italian and art history, and visit the major museums in the city as well as Venice, Siena, and Pisa.

Price includes:

Accommodations, some meals, transportation, tuition, excursions, ESA activities, entry fees, international student ID card.

Sample trips:

$2,275 for five weeks in Tokyo.
$2,355 for four weeks in Paris, full board.
$3,475 for semester in Florence.

SAN JOSE STATE UNIVERSITY

Address: International Travel Programs
Office of Continuing Education
Administration Building 104
San Jose, CA 95192-0135
Phone: (408)924-2680
Fax: (408)924-2666
Contact: Judy Rickard

"Any adult interested in a study vacation or a travel program with an academic interest is a candidate for our year-round programs," notes Judy Rickard.

A 64-page booklet lists the dozens of trips offered to Ecuador, Kenya, Nepal, Morocco, Egypt, Thailand, London, and Mexico among others. The courses include field trips, lectures, discussions, seminars, and individual study projects. Students are expected to complete academic assignments and pre-travel reading. The trips have been approved by the university, meet the same academic standards established on campus, and are led by qualified academic escorts.

Each program has a particular focus. Dr. Barbara Joans leads an exploration of Alaska's Inside Passage waterway amid glacial ice and rugged mountains; she's a cultural anthropologist who has lived among Native American peoples and written about their lives for several years.

The program in Russia, in which participants are "adopted" by a Russian families in Tbilisi and visit their homes, workplaces, and schools, is led by Dr. Ronald Hideo Hayashida, an associate professor of comparative politics at Ramapo College of New Jersey who spent a year on the Historical Faculty of Moscow University.

The London theaters program is led by Professor Donamarie Reeds of the SJSU Theatre Arts Department, a scenic designer, actress, and director.

Price includes:

Airfare from California, accommodations, some meals, transportation, sightseeing, interpreters, admission fees, health/accident insurance, tuition, packet of information.

Sample trips:

$1,451 for a week in London.
$2,662 for four weeks, language and culture in France.
$3,185 for two weeks in Ecuador/Galapagos Islands.

One participant commented: "I found the group to be excellent traveling companions as they tended to want an educational dimension like myself. They asked intelligent questions and were extremely congenial."

SCANDINAVIAN SEMINAR

Address: **24 Dickinson Street**
Amherst, MA 01002
Phone: **(413)253-9736**
Contact: **Mary Schnackenberg Cattani, Executive Director**

Since 1949, thousands of undergraduates, graduates, and other adults have successfully taken part in the Scandinavian Seminar by living and studying in Norway, Sweden, Finland, or Denmark in the Total Immersion Year Abroad program. Students learn the language and live and attend classes at a Folk College with other Scandinavian students. The Seminar places participants individually in some 45 to 60 folk colleges each year.

One student commented: "The amazing, exhilarating part is that I now feel natural speaking Swedish. I remember thinking in October that I would just learn more and more words, but never feel comfortable when I spoke. Now I enjoy speaking in Swedish."

For students who do not have the time to spend a year in Denmark, Sweden, Norway or Finland, the Scandinavian Seminar also offers fall and spring semester programs on Nordic and global issues at Folk Colleges.

Price includes:

Accommodation, meals, a family stay, tuition, language instruction, group seminars in three countries.

Sample trips:

$10,900 for one-year program.
$6,000 to $6,500 for four-month fall/spring semesters.

A student wrote: "I've learned something I never expected to learn about while I was abroad, and that is my own country. The value of learning to look at one's own country objectively is incomparable."

SIERRA CLUB

Address: **730 Polk Street**
San Francisco, CA 94109
Phone: **(415)776-2211**
Contact: **Director, Outing Department**

The Sierra Club has been in the outdoor education business for over 100 years. Founded by John Muir to preserve the wilderness of the West, its thousands of members work for laws to keep the air and water clean, preserve national parks and wilderness areas, take action against destructive development, and travel into wilderness, parks, and forests to enjoy nature.

Every year, *Sierra* magazine lists hundreds of backpacking, hiking, trekking, biking, boating, and skiing trips in the United States and abroad. More than 3,500 men, women, and children take part in them.

All Sierra tours promote an understanding of environmental issues and use minimum-impact camping techniques. Trips are graded Light, Moderate or Strenuous, or a combination of several levels. Beginners can enjoy a leisurely week's backpack with short day hikes and rest days for fishing, photography, and relaxation. More experienced hikers climb up 14,000-foot peaks or trek off the trail across the rocks and cliffs of the Grand Canyon Park, Arizona. Several trips explore Alaska, including a fishing trip.

You can choose Service Trips, on which members work on clearing and rebuilding hiking trails; stay at a Base Camp and take day hikes; or join a Burro Trip where mules carry the baggage. There are also Family Outings, specially designed for parents and children.

Foreign trips to Asia, Africa, India, and China, among others, can include camping in remote areas or staying in guest houses or hotels. Participants often learn about conservation problems and meet local environmentalists. In 1990, there's a hiking trip to Russia along the borders of China and Afghanistan amid some of the highest mountains in the world.

Price includes:

Accommodations, transportation to and from meeting point, all meals, guides, instruction, facilities.

Sample trips:

$290 for seven days backpacking, Yosemite, California.
$650 for eight days, base camp, Pecos Wilderness, New Mexico.
$995 for 14 days backpacking, Arctic Wildlife Refuge, Alaska.
$2,350 for 14 days walking in Lake District, England.

"We had a wonderful time on the Finger Lakes Toddler Tromp," noted a hiker. "Our family left the city and our routine hassles far behind within hours of arriving at camp."

SLICKROCK ADVENTURES

Address: PO Box 1400
Moab UT 84532
Phone: (801)259-6996
Fax: (801)259-8698
Contact: Cully Erdman

Kayaking and paddle-rafting adventures on both river and sea, as well as mountain bike trips in Utah's canyonlands, are offered by this company, founded in 1970. The trips blend instruction and active involvement, so that participants learn new skills and enjoy them.

In Mexico, there are raft and kayak trips down the Chancala, Jatate, and Usumacinta Rivers in the Chiapas region, where the adventure movie *Romancing The Stone* was shot. All the rivers wind through tropical rain forests, where travelers hear the squawks of parrots and macaws and glimpse monkeys, cotamundi and deer amid the foliage.

In Baja California, there are week-long excursions exploring the coastline near Loreto, a rugged shore with rocks and bays. And in Belize, participants kayak along a barrier reef 20 miles offshore, accompanied by a local fisherman/diver who provides fish for meals; there's also camping on reef islands and unsurpassed snorkeling.

Price includes:

Accommodations, all meals, transportation, kayaks, rafts, accessories, guides and instruction.

Sample trips:

$795 for seven-day kayak trips in Baja California.
$925 for seven-day kayak trips in Belize.
$875 to $1,195 for eight to 13 days, kayak/raft, Mexico.

SMITHSONIAN STUDY TOURS

Address: 1100 Jefferson Drive, SW
Washington DC 20560
Phone: (202)357-4700
Fax: (202)786-2315
Contact: Prudence Clendenning, Deputy Manager

The Smithsonian National Associates Program has long been recognized as the leader in study tours and expeditions. Over 160 study tours and seminars led by outstanding experts in their field are offered year-round and range from the California gold rush to English gardens, from wildlife to sculpture, from baseball stadiums to Christmas in Switzerland.

Their Domestic Study Tours include visits to the Grand Canyon, Baja California for whale watching, spring gardens in Washington DC and Delaware, tours of Hawaii, the Everglades in Florida and New York City's Art Deco.

Foreign Study Tours include a cruise through the Caribbean aboard the *Sea Cloud*, a sailing ship built for a millionaire couple; and a tour to Russia to attend concerts by the Leningrad Philharmonic, dance performances by the Maly Theater ballet company, and a tour of the glories of the Hermitage. There are safaris to Kenya and Tanzania, a journey down the Nile River, and an exploration of the culture of Jamaica.

Research expeditions take participants to work with scientists on projects such as monitoring volcano eruptions in Costa Rica, studying extinct plants in the fossil forests of Wyoming, and documenting the Annual Crow Fair in Billings, Montana.

New Winter Interludes tours visit different cities during the off-season to experience the ambience of the place without the summer tourists. In November, participants go to Venice and see the art collection of Peggy Guggenheim, and in February they explore Prague with a visit to Prague's Jewish Museum.

A dozen Countryside Tours offer travelers the chance to spend two weeks in one place as part of their trip. These include visiting the village of St. Davids in Wales where Welsh is still spoken; staying in Randers in Denmark with its storks nests, timber-framed houses and cobble-stoned streets; or exploring Sopran, a 900-year-old town in Hungary in the foothills of the Alps.

Price includes:

Airfare, accommodations, some meals, excursions, transportation, guides.

Sample trips:

$995 for a week touring the Everglades, Florida.
$1,125 for two weeks work in fossil forests, Wyoming.
$2,990 for 10 days in Venice.
$3,635 for two weeks in Wales.

"We were treated as friends and colleagues," noted a woman on a Smithsonian research program. "The scientists went out of their way to be sure the volunteers got the most out of the program."

SOBEK EXPEDITIONS

Address: **PO Box 1089**
Angels Camp CA 95222
Phone: **(209)777-7939**
Fax: **(209)736-2646**
Contact: **Information Office**

Sobek Expeditions, established in 1976, publishes a 94-page full-color catalog listing their scores of adventurous journeys to Asia, Africa, South America, the Middle East, Indian, Nepal, Tibet, Thailand, Europe, Alaska, Australia, New Zealand, New Guinea, the Andes, and Antarctica.

The company has created a Code of Adventure Travel Ethics, emphasizing: "We must always remember we are visitors on others' soil, and we must tread carefully."

The Code points suggest the following:

- Travel in a spirit of humility and with a genuine desire to learn more about the people of your host country.
- Cultivate the habit of listening and observing.
- Acquaint yourself with local customs.
- Remember that you are only one of thousands of tourists visiting this country, and do not expect special privileges.
- When you are shopping, remember that the "bargain" you obtained was possible because of the low wages paid to the maker.
- Do not make promises to people in your host country unless you can carry them through.

Sobek trips are active participatory experiences, with ballooning, skin diving, hiking, trekking, rafting, sailing, cycling, and more. Over 100 expeditions are offered year-round.

You can join a wildlife safari in Tanzania, go on an exploration of Madagascar, take a jungle trek on the Kokoda Trail in Papua New Guinea, choose a rafting and trekking excursion in Kashmir, ride a bicycle through China, sail around the Great Barrier Reef of Australia, or try a walking tour of the Alps in Switzerland, among dozens of others. The company arranges custom travel trips on request.

Price includes:

Airfare, accommodations, all meals, transportation, guides, fees.

Sample trips:

$2,295 for two weeks in Costa Rica.
$3,950 for 20 days in India and Nepal.
$5,195 for 14 days rafting in Soviet Union.

SOCIETY EXPEDITIONS

Address: 3131 Elliott Avenue, Suite 700
Seattle WA 98121
Phone: (206)285-9400
Fax: (206)285-7917
Contact: Kathleen Dunlap, Director of Public Relations

This company began in 1974 as the Society for the Preservation of Archeological Monuments. Several groups were taken to Easter Island with an archaeologist as leader, and all profits from the trips were given to help restore the island's giant statues. In 1976, Society Expeditions was created.

Today, descriptions of the cruises it offers on its two ships fill 120 pages of a glossy full-color catalog. These include exploring the Antarctic continent from Australia and New Zealand, discovering the headhunting tribes of Indonesia New Guinea's Asmat region, visiting the palm-fringed beaches of the Marquesas Islands in the South Pacific, and sailing around the Canadian Arctic and Greenland waterways to Hudson Bay.

The emphasis is educational. Every passenger receives a notebook with essays, graphs, maps, and illustrations related to their destination, as well as a reading list. At the end of the trip, participants receive a bound logbook of their adventure.

Experts give shipboard lectures and discuss the history, geology, culture, and wildlife of the region. Experienced naturalists lead shore excursions. Passengers are briefed on conservation and warned to be careful about wandering from paths; not to touch wildlife; never to bring skins, bones, eggs or any part of protected animal species aboard; and to carry all litter back to the ship.

"Our goal is to set a good example for our travelers and the world community," said James Claus, the head of Society Expeditions. "We want our ships to be recognized as permanent symposiums on conservation and welcomed as ambassadors of conservation at every destination we visit."

Price includes:

Accommodations, all meals, shore excursions, guides, transportation, lectures, notebooks, logs, all tips, port and airport taxes. Range of prices reflects cabin choice.

Sample trips:

$3,990 to $7,550 for 12 days on Upper Amazon.
$5,390 to $10,600 for 15 days in Marquesas Islands.
$6,290 to $10,690 for 15 days in Antarctica.
$14,250 to $25,990 for 30 days in Antarctica.

SPECIAL ODYSSEYS/ARCTIC

Address: Box 37
Medina WA 98039
Phone: (206)455-1960
Contact: Susan Voorhees

A pioneering company in the exploration of the Arctic, Special Odysseys offers adventures at the North and South Poles, the most isolated points of the world. The trips are led by educational experts or by experienced Eskimos of the Inuit tribe.

"The Arctic displays an awesome vastness and breathtaking beauty to those who visit," says a staff member. "The abundance of wildflowers and lichen in this land of endless quiet adds another dimension, of contrast, color, and delicacy. And it's a rare opportunity to see at close hand polar bears, wolves, caribou, narwhal and beluga whales, musk oxen, and other species in their natural environment."

On the eight day North Pole journey from Canada, participants visit a scientific station in the Arctic, travel to the most northerly lake in the world, and visit Grise Fjord with its spectacular glaciers to take snowmobile rides up the face of the glacier and down its convex cliffs.

The South Pole trip flies to the Thiel Mountains, with snow-tractor rides to explore the region, lectures on history and natural sciences, and, if weather permits, a flight to the South Pole.

In Canada's Northwest Territories, weekly Dog Sled runs led by an Eskimo Inuit guide are offered, speeding along the edge of the ice floes where polar bears, walruses, seals, beluga whales, and narwhals congregate. Participants sleep in tents or Eskimo igloos made of snow.

Special Odyssey trips are frequently arranged for groups with an interest in wildlife, ornithology, photography, native cultures or history.

Price includes:

Airfare from Ottawa or Montreal, accommodations, all meals, transportation, guides, excursions.

Sample trips:

$2,800 for nine-day Dog Sled trip.
$3,990 for 10-day Worlds of the High Arctic trip.
$7,900 for seven-day North Pole trip from Resolute Bay, Canada.
$30,000 for two-weeks trip to South Pole from Chile.

STANFORD ALUMNI ASSOCIATION

Address: **Travel/Study Programs**
Stanford University
Bowman Alumni House
Stanford, CA 94305-4005
Phone: **(415)725-1093**
Fax: **(415)725-8675**
Contact: **Mev Hoberg, Reservations Coordinator**

Stanford's travel programs are open to alumni, their families, and friends of the university. Dozens of trips are offered throughout the year.

"On every trip, you travel with a faculty leader who is an expert on some aspect of the place you visit," Peter R. Voll, Director of the Travel/Study Programs explains. "Stanford's top archaeologists, engineers, marine geologists, biologists, historians, political scientists, and others give lectures and more informally walk and talk with you throughout your travels."

In the United States, study tours steam up the Mississippi River in an old-fashioned paddle boat; explore the Southwest to visit the Hopi Indian potters and basket makers, Zuni silversmiths, and Navajo weavers; and go river-running through the Grand Canyon.

In Europe, there's a Dutch Waterways College which floats down the canals from Zipje to Arnhem with stops to taste cheese in Gouda, view Van Gogh drawings in Otterlo, and stroll through Volendam, where people wear local costumes and wooden shoes. There's a Walking Tour of Tuscany covering about 10 miles a day between picturesque Italian villages, with wine-tasting and delicious meals along the way. And Anglophiles may enjoy a seminar at Brasenose College, Oxford, with lectures, high tea, and boating on the Thames.

Price includes:

Accommodations, meals, transportation, tuition, excursions, guides.

Sample trips:

$1,200 for nine days, Salmon River Expedition, Idaho.
$1,900 for eight days on Bonaire Snorkeling Expedition.
$3,300 for 14 days, Oxford/Stanford Seminar, England.

"We loved the wonderful group, and the gorgeous countryside we saw," said a woman who took a canal trip through Provence and the south of France. "It was like drifting through a painting for hours at a time."

STATE UNIVERSITY OF NEW YORK

Address: International Education Office
College of New Paltz
HAB 33/SUNY New Paltz
New Paltz, NY 12561
Phone: (914)257-3125
Contact: Mary Collins-Bastian,
Assistant Director

The International Education Office offers students the chance to spend a summer, a semester, or an academic year abroad in China, England, France, Germany, Italy, Spain, Russia or Israel.

In China, there's an academic year abroad program offered in Beijing, with Chinese-language courses at various levels, lodging in university dormitories, and field trips and cultural programs. Two years of college-level Chinese is required.

In Europe, students can spend a semester or the academic year in France, Italy, or Spain taking courses in language and literature as well as history and culture. Students live in dorms or with families, and several field trips are included.

There's a London Theatre Seminar in January, with lectures, workshops, talks by visiting artists, and informal meetings with actors. Semester Seminars in England include art history, American studies, geography, law, philosophy, and more.

In the summer, there's a six week program in France with half the time in Besancon and half in Paris. Other summer programs run in Ovideo, Spain, and in Hamburg, Germany. There are also several seminars in Russia with language courses, field trips, and cultural events in Lvov, Kalinen, or Leningrad; participants must be under 40.

In 1990, the International Relations Program and the Department of Political Science plan a summer study tour to

Israel, to meet with Israeli and Palestinian leaders, journalists, and scholars, and to explore the Israeli-Palestinian conflict and the role of geography in Israeli security.

Price includes:

Airfare, accommodations, some meals, transportation, tuition, excursions, guides.

Sample trips:

$1,800 for two weeks in Israel.
$3,500 for three-month semester in France.
$5,000 for summer in Leningrad.
$9,000 for academic year in China; New York state students.

SUN VALLEY TREKKING COMPANY

Address: **Box 2200**
Sun Valley ID 83353
Phone: **(208)788-9585**
Contact: **Bob Jonas**

This commercial adventure company provides a strong educational emphasis for its skiing and trekking trips around Idaho.

"Our back-country ski adventures let participants become familiar with the nature of the white wilderness through professional naturalist-guides," explains Bob Jonas. "We share our knowledge and that includes everything from snow-pack dynamics to avalanche awareness to winter ecology principles."

Sun Valley's trips explore Monolith Valley, Thompson Peak in the Sawtooth Mountains, and Yellowstone National Park. Participants can try alpine skiing on Idaho's Mt. Baldy, spend an evening ski touring to a Mongul yurt for dinner, enjoy ski tours into the backcountry, or ski-trek for several days and camp out in the wilderness. There are also cross-country ski tours from hut-to-hut, where travelers can help with the cooking and carry the food, or, if they prefer, they can travel with a chef who prepares meals while guides carry the gear.

The company designs "The Best of Sun Valley" ski packages, with alpine and cross-country skiing and backcountry excursions. Their "Total Skiing" package offers 10 days of skiing, films, and clinics.

Price includes:

Accommodations, meals, guides and usually equipment.

Sample trips:

$45 for evening ski to Mongolian yurt for dinner.
$55 for one-day backcountry ski clinic.
$110 per day for hut-to-hut catered ski tour.
$525 for seven-day ski trekking, Sawtooth Haute Route, Idaho.

SYRACUSE UNIVERSITY

Address: **International Programs Abroad**
119 Euclid Avenue
Syracuse NY 13244
Phone: **(315)443-9420**
Fax: **(315)443-4593**
Contact: **Lynn Cavicchi, Summer Program Coordinator**

Syracuse University has a wide selection of summer travel and study programs designed mainly for mature learners, but they are open to graduate and undergraduate students too.

The tour to the Soviet Union takes only 12 participants. Led by John Hodgson, professor of political science at Syracuse, it includes a week's study in London followed by a tour of Russia with stops in Moscow, Tibilisi, and Tallinn.

A European tour explores Holland and France in the footsteps of Vincent Van Gogh, with visits to the Rijksmuseum in Amsterdam and the Louvre in Paris. And a food-lovers' tour of France tastes the regional cuisines of Strasbourg, Champagne, Avignon, and Alsace.

Particularly popular is a Medieval Pilgrimage Routes program which follows the path 12th century religious pilgrims walked from Arles in southeastern France to Santiago de Compostela in northwest Spain. The tour is led by Professor William Melczer and his assistant Elisabeth Kaltenbrunner-Melczer, who lecture on the monuments and works of art along the way. The Scandinavian Smorgasbord tour visits Finland, Sweden, Norway, and Denmark.

For graduates and undergraduates, the university offers summer internships in fashion design and in management and courses in TV and radio drama, marketing strategies, politics, and retailing in Britain; a travel program on architecture in Stuttgart, Germany, emphasizing Rococo and NeoClassicist styles; and a program in Strasbourg, France, which explores history, political science, and engineering. Students can earn experience credit at the Council of Europe as well as taking French-language classes. There are additional programs in Italy and Switzerland.

Price includes:

Airfare from New York, transfers, accommodations, breakfast, some meals, transportation, field trips, tours, entry fees.

Sample trips:

$2,195 for 16 days, Medieval Pilgrimage.
$2,975 for 17 days, Scandinavian Smorgasbord tour.
$3,350 for 20 days, Gastronomie Fantastique in France.
$3,800 for two weeks in England and the Soviet Union.

TEXAS CAMEL CORPS AT THE WITTE MUSEUM

Address: San Antonio Museum Association
PO Box 2601
San Antonio TX 78299-2601
Phone: (512)226-5544
Fax: (512)824-1400
Contact: Ian P. McCord, Director of Travel

The original Texas Camel Corps was created in the 1830s, when a group of intrepid Army officers shipped a herd of camels into Texas from Saudi Arabia. The adventurous soldiers hoped to provide a means of transportation across the arid deserts of the Southwest. But the Civil War and the expanding railroads ended the experiment, and the camels ran wild before dying out in the 1880s.

The Witte Museum's Texas Camel Corps began in 1985. Its goal is to explore and enjoy the remote regions of Texas and beyond. You can join as a Founder for $100 or as a Private First Class for $20 plus a membership fee to the San Antonio Museum Association; if you live more than 50 miles outside the city, you pay $25.

Members enjoy discounts on TCC trips as well as in restaurants and shops in San Antonio. They can attend events and monthly meetings at the Witte Museum, and they receive a lively newsletter from TCC Brigadier-General in Charge Ian P. McCord.

Trips include weekend outings to the National Wildlife Refuge on the Gulf Coast, where the last truly wild population of whooping cranes lives; a tour of Lower Pecos Prehistoric Indian Rock Shelters in Texas; or whale-watching in the Pacific.

Traveling abroad, TCC members go hiking in Copper Canyon, Mexico, and further afield to explore Egypt, Nepal, Brazil, and Ecuador. Non-members are welcome on all trips.

Price includes:

Airfare, accommodations, meals, transportation, guides.

Sample trips:

$79 for two-day trip to see whooping cranes, Gulf Coast.
$1,685 for eight-day whale-watching cruise, Baja California.
$3,775 for 18 days in India and Nepal.

TEXTILE MUSEUM

Address: **2320 S Street NW**
Washington DC 20008
Phone: **(202)667-0442/(703)920-0228**
Contact: **Margot Phillips, Travel Manager**

The Textile Museum is the only museum in the Western Hemisphere devoted solely to the conservation, acquisition, and exhibition of rugs and textiles.

Its unique shows have included "Molas of the Kuna Indians," displaying woven designs created by the 25,000 Indians on small islands along the northeast coast of Panama; and "Dragons, Blossoms, Sunbursts: Textile Arts of the Caucasus," with vividly patterned rugs made in the mountainous regions between the Black and Caspian Seas in Russia.

The museum's travel programs naturally focus on textiles. There's a tour of Coptic and Pharonic textiles in Cairo and a cruise to the 3,000 islands of Indonesia with a noted leader of Indonesian textiles. Other tours explore the Hatay region of Turkey between Antakya and Trabzon to see Reyhanli kilims and vivid Malatya weavings.

In France, Jean-Michel Tuchscherer, former curator of the Musee des Arts Decoratif in Lyons, leads the group to see the textiles and rugs of Alsace, Paris, Tours, Angers, Aubusson, and Lyons, with special visits to private chateaux.

Price includes:

Airfare, accommodations, some meals, transportation, guides, airport taxes, entrance fees, and a $300 contribution to the Textile Museum.

Sample trip:

$4,000 for 14 days in Egypt.

TOLEDO MUSEUM OF ART

Address: **PO Box 1013**
Toledo OH 43697
Phone: **(419)255-8000**
Fax: **(419)255-5638**
Contact: **David W. Steadman, Director**

Museum members—it costs $30 a year to join—take art-related weekend trips to New York, Chicago, Winterthur in Delaware, Santa Fe, Detroit, Cleveland, and Columbus. There's one annual trip abroad.

In 1990, participants travel to Spain, led by two professors from the art department of the University of Toledo. The tour begins in Catalonia in the northeast and travels south to reach Castille and Madrid. Along the way, there'll be visits to Burgos, Leon, Santiago de Compostela and Segovia, and guided tours of the Picasso Museum in Barcelona, the Castle of Cardona, and the Prado Museum in Madrid.

The group is limited to 30 people. Participants attend a pre-trip lecture and receive a reading list beforehand.

Price includes:

Airfare, transportation, accommodations, most meals, guides, plus $350 contribution to Toledo Museum of Art.

Sample trip:

$4,500 for 17 days in Spain.

TOWSON STATE UNIVERSITY

Address: **Modern Languages Department**
Towson MD 21204
Phone: **(301)830-2883**
Contact: **Dr. Jorge A. Giro**

The university offers summer travel-study programs in Spain. One trips spends eight days in Madrid and six days touring the region of Andalucia. On the 29-day trip, students attend Spanish-language and conversation classes in Madrid and then spend six days touring Cordoba, Granada, and the Costa del Sol in Andalucia.

"Our summer program is designed to provide the best learning experience about the Spanish life and culture," notes Dr. Giro. Classes are taught by native Spanish speakers with credentials from American and Spanish universities.

Participants live in a student residence at the Cuidad Universitaria in Madrid, and all meals are provided in the official dining room of the Colegio Mayor. Classes are held in the Colegio Mayor and in the Prado Museum in Madrid.

Price includes:

Airfare from New York, accommodations, all meals, tuition, transportation, and excursions.

Sample trips:

$1,495 for 14-day trip in Spain.
$1,995 for 29-day trip in Spain.

TULANE UNIVERSITY

Address: **Summer School**
125 Gibson Hall
New Orleans, LA 70118
Phone: **(504)865-5555**
Contact: **Amy Pick**

The university offers Summer Abroad programs in Paris, Tokyo, Mexico City, and Cambridge, England.

The Paris program schedules morning classes in art history, the French language, and political science. Afternoons are free, and several excursions are offered in and around the city, with a special trip to Mont St. Michel on the coast of Normandy.

In Tokyo, students live in international student dormitories a short subway ride from Sophia University. Their Asian studies program includes courses on Japanese art, the rise of Japanese industry, Japanese management, religions, language, and literature.

Price includes:

Airfare, accommodations, some meals, orientation, excursions, tuition, credits.

Sample trips:

$3,725 for six weeks, Summer Abroad in Paris.
$5,545 for six weeks, Summer Abroad in Tokyo.

UNITED STATES-CHINA PEOPLES FRIENDSHIP ASSOCIATION

Address: **Western Region Office**
50 Oak Street, Room 502
San Francisco CA 94102
Phone: **(415)863-0537**
Contact: **Christine Kelley**

USCPFA, which has 60 local chapters across the United States, provides cultural programs, speakers, and films on life in China; organizes social events for local Chinese students and scholars; and publishes the *US-China Review* for its members. It also offers language and cultural tours in China.

Since 1972, its study tours to China have been designed to help Americans understand Chinese social life and culture through people-to-people contact.

Students can take intensive language programs in the summer and fall in China at the Beijing Language Institute, with classes five days a week for a couple of months followed by two weeks of travel around the country.

A different educational tours sends students to Qufu for a week. Qufu was the home of Confucius and offers a unique view of life in a small northern country town. Participants attend language classes and lectures on Chinese history, health, family life, literature, painting, music, food, and shadow boxing. Then there are two weeks of travel to Shanghai, Suzhou, Wuxi, Xuzhou, Jinan, and Beijing.

Price includes:

Airfare from San Francisco, accommodations, transportation, meals, tuition.

Sample trips:

$2,390 for 18-day tour of China.
$3,160 for eight weeks of language study in China.
$3,350 for 10 weeks of language study in China.

One participant commented: "I will long remember Qufu, where in Spring the sycamore trees line the main street, where blue clad peasant farmers mingle with students, and where small shops along the main street are interspersed with carts displaying spring vegetables from the fields. Birds in bamboo cages adorn stalls while child-sized tables and chairs offer a place to have a morning meal of hot rice cereal and an oval doughnut."

UNITED STATES-JAPAN CROSS CULTURE CENTER

Address: **244 S San Pedro St., Suite 305**
Los Angeles CA 90012
Phone: **(213)617-2039**
Fax: **(213)680-4531**
Contact: **Greg Golley**

"We are an educational center that provides scholarships, workshops, and seminars for people interested in learning about, studying, or working in Japan," explains a staff member.

The Center has offices in Los Angeles and New York and sponsors seminars and classes in Japanese and language teaching, home-stay and study programs in Japan, and a workshop on living and traveling in Japan. It also publishes

Japan Journal magazine, provides translation and interpretive services, and has a reference library open to the public. It offers travel programs in cooperation with the Tokyo-based Inter-Cultural Institute of Japan.

The Home-stay and Study program brings participants to Tokyo for two or three weeks to live with a Japanese family, attend language lessons, and go on trips and excursions. Longer programs of a month or more add additional classes in Japanese language and culture. Scholarships are available for those who want to spend a year studying in Japan.

Price includes:

Accommodations, all meals, registration, tuition, field trips, sayonara dinner.

Sample trips:

$1,000 for two weeks, home-stay and study in Japan.
$1,200 for three weeks, home-stay and study in Japan.

UNIVERSITY OF CALIFORNIA /BERKELEY

Address: **Marketing Dept. 5A**
2223 Fulton Street
Berkeley CA 94720
Phone: **(415)642-4111**
Fax: **(415)643-8683**
Contact: **Lynne Kaufman, Program Director**

Students, professionals, and retirees join UC/Berkeley tours to Europe. One of the most popular is the joint summer program with Oxford University, England with courses on Chaucer and the Middle Ages, The Evolution of the English Village, The Novel and Society, and England in the Age of the Stuarts.

Students have access to the university libraries, the museums, and the gardens of the college. The program began in 1979 and more than 4,000 people have participated.

Berkeley also offers a program in London on the theater, in Scotland on its history and culture including attendance at the Edinburgh Festival, on modern art in the south of France, and in Italy, on art, architecture and history.

A three weeks program in Paris enables students to live in a residence hall near the Bois de Boulogne and attend courses on French art and culture.

Price includes:

Accommodations, all meals, tuition.

Sample trips:

$2,600 for two weeks in France, studying modern art.
$2,700 for three weeks in Florence and Tuscany.
$4,100 for six weeks at Oxford University.

A professor from South Africa who joined the Oxford University program commented: "It was an unforgettable experience especially as it took place in such beautiful surroundings." And a woman from Dallas, Texas noted: "I enjoyed the opportunity to visit with other people across the country who are intellectually curious. It was a most delightful mix of age groups."

UNIVERSITY OF CALIFORNIA/ LOS ANGELES

Address: 10995 LeConte, Suite 315
Los Angeles CA 90024
Phone: (213)825-1901
Fax: (213)206-5123
Contact: John Watson, Public Information Representative

UCLA Extension attracts travelers aged 18 to 80 who join study tours to the Amazon, Antarctica, Mexico, Turkey, Egypt, and Cambridge University, England, among others.

Edwin C. Krupp, Director of the Griffith Park Observatory in Los Angeles, leads the UCLA tour of the Yucatan Peninsula, which explores Mayan ruins for signs of ancient astronomy. In the Amazon basin tour, the group is headed by two UCLA professors and travels to Tampobata Nature Reserve, Cuzco and Machu Picchu.

Egyptian archeologist Dr. Zahi Howass leads the tour in Egypt, where participants visit sites not normally open to the public, including the new excavations at Luxor and recently discovered royal tombs.

In England, there are seminars at Cambridge University on topics such as British landscapes and gardens, Dickens and the Victorian era, and Winston Churchill and his times.

A special Midsummer in London seminar offers a Festival of International Theatre acting workshop. Students and professionals work with actors and directors from four leading theatre companies. There are also classes in voice, movement, and mime. Admission is by audition only.

Price includes:

Accommodations, all meals, transportation, tuition.

Sample trips:

$2,525 for 10 days in Yucatan Peninsula.
$2,695 for three weeks at Cambridge University.
$3,830 for 23 days in the Amazon.
$3,700 for 17 days in Egypt, including airfare.

UNIVERSITY OF CALIFORNIA/SANTA CRUZ

Address: **740 Front Street**
Santa Cruz CA 95060
Phone: **(408)427-6620**
Fax: **(408)427-6608**
Contact: **Travel Director**

Photography is a special interest of the UC/Santa Cruz programs. Weekend photography workshops are taught by outstanding photographers and educators at a variety of locations including Point Reyes, Monterey, the Mono Basin, the Mojave Desert, Yosemite, and Death Valley in California. There's also a traveling photographic workshop in southern France.

Workshops take place outdoors and are rarely canceled because of bad weather: "In many cases, this is an integral part of the visual experience offered," explains the director.

Other arts-related trips include a tour of Russia and a course of landscape painting in north Wales.

Price includes:

Tuition only. Participants provide their own photographic equipment, and usually make their own arrangements for food, lodging, or camping.

Sample trips:

$140 for weekend photo workshop in Point Reyes, California.

$280 for weekend photo workshop in Yosemite, with lodging.

UNIVERSITY OF DETROIT

Address: **Classic Theatre Program**
Theatre Department
4001 W McNichols Road
Detroit MI 48221
Phone: **(313)927-1514**
Contact: **Dr. Arthur J. Beer**

A classic theatre program in Greece with daily voice, movement, and acting workshops is conducted by experienced professionals during June on the island of Spetse.

Following a three-week rehearsal period in residence, the company tours a new production of a classic comedy or tragedy to both ancient and modern amphitheaters. During the tour week, the company also visits classic sites and attends a production by the Greek National Theatre.

"The theatre program was designed for our own pre-professional undergraduates," explains Dr. Beer, "but it has attracted the attention of several professional performers."

In 1989, a new rock musical version of Aristophanes' *The Birds* was presented to enthusiastic reviews. In 1990, the show will be revived, and there will be the premiere of an operatic version of *Agamemnon*.

Price includes:

Airfare, accommodations, two meals a day, transportation, lectures, workshops, admissions to sites and productions.

Sample trips:

$2,300 for participants under age 25.
$2,500 for participants over age 25.

UNIVERSITY OF NEW ORLEANS

Address: **Office of International Study Programs**
Metropolitan College
New Orleans LA 70148
Phone: **(504)286-7318**
Fax: **(504)286-7363**
Contact: **William Carl Wagner**

The cornerstone of UNO's international study program is its successful relationship with the University of Innsbruck in Austria. The university, located amid the spectacular mountains of the Tyrolean Alps on the banks of the Inn River, has signed a Friendship Treaty with UNO and six other universities so that UNO students are accepted at Innsbruck. The Innsbruck University buildings are a few minutes walk from the "Old City," which dates back to Roman times. The town is within easy reach of Munich, Salzburg, Vienna, Venice, Florence, and Rome.

Students can take courses during the academic year, the fall or spring semesters, the international summer school, or special summer seminars for adults. UNO, in cooperation with the University of New Hampshire, also offers Interhostel programs.

More than 3,000 college, high-school, and adult students have enrolled in Innsbruck programs since 1975.

Other programs include summer study in French in Montpellier for high-school students, undergraduates, graduates, and adults. Montpellier is a few miles from the beaches of the Mediterranean and reflects the culture and ambience of the south of France. Daily French classes use the audiovisual method developed by professors at the Universite Paul Valery Montpellier III.

In the Italian Alps, anthropology seminars are offered at the Ezra Pound Center for Anthropology in Brunnenburg Castle, which belongs to Ezra Pound's grandson, an anthropologist. Students live in a 17th century farmhouse within the castle complex and work in the museum and village nearby. Also available in July is a course on the literature of Ezra Pound.

In Belgium, participants work on restoring a splendid medieval chateau abandoned after World War II. In England, they attend a seminar for teachers, prospective teachers, and administrators on elementary instruction in British and American schools.

Price includes:

Accommodations, all meals, tuition, books, insurance, activities, facilities.

Sample trips:

$1,199 for four weeks at Havre, Belgium.
$1,399 for four weeks at Ezra Pound Center, Italy.
$2,495 for six weeks at summer school, Innsbruck.
$9,900 for academic year at Innsbruck; includes airfare.

UNIVERSITY OF RHODE ISLAND

Address: **Summer Program in Spain**
Department of Languages
Kingston RI 02881
Phone: **(401)792-4717**
Contact: **Prof. Mario F. Trubiano, Director**

Intensive language and cultural programs, as well as a graduate program leading to a master's degree in Hispanic Studies, are offered by the University of Rhode Island in collaboration with the Colegio de Espana in Salamanca, Spain.

The four week summer courses offer 25 hours a week of classroom instruction, four hours a week of language practice and 30 hours of excursions and cultural activities. There are two critics-in-residence on hand to answer questions about Spanish literature, society, and culture. Students live in dormitories on campus.

Students join excursions to Segovia, Madrid, Toledo, Escorial, and Cuenca as well as to Leon, Zamora, Avila, Alba de Tormes, and the Andalucian region of Seville, Cordoba, and Granada.

Price includes:

Accommodations, all meals, transportation, tuition, cultural activities, three excursions with guide, language practice, parties.

Sample trip:

$1,125 for four week session in Spain.

UNIVERSITY OF SOUTHWESTERN LOUISIANA

Address: USL France
USL Box 43331
Lafayette LA 70504
Phone: (318)231-5449/6811
Fax: (318)231-6195
Contact: Frans C. Amelinckx

The shimmering blue Mediterranean in the south of France, and the hazy purple peaks of the mountains inland provide an idyllic setting for USL summer language courses for graduate and undergraduate students and adult auditors. Subjects include French, anthropology, economics, creative writing, management, marketing, physics, and art taught by USL faculty in English.

Classes are given at the Institut Franco-Europeen in Juan-les-Pins, located near Nice. The town is a typical French seaside resort with a magnificent sandy beach, sports facilities, the famous Grimaldi Palace Museum with its Picasso exhibition, and a lively nightlife.

Students live in double rooms in a comfortable university residence, with meals during the week in the Institute diningroom or on the palm terrace outside. Table wine is served with lunch and dinner.

Classes run Monday through Thursday, so students can take trips over the weekend to explore the regions of Provence and Burgundy as well as Switzerland and northern Italy. Several excursions, including a week in Paris, are included.

Price includes:

Airfare, accommodations, most meals, transportation, tuition, excursions, fees, insurance.

Sample trip:

$3,800 for six weeks in Juan-les-Pins and Antibes plus week in Paris.

UNIVERSITY OF TENNESSEE

Address: Graphic Design in London
Department of Art
1715 Volunteer Boulevard
Knoxville TN 37996-2410
Phone: (615)974-3408
Fax: (615)974-8546
Contact: Professors William Kennedy and Susan E. Metros

A month-long summer course in British graphic design is offered to students and professional designers. Organized by the Department of Art and the University Evening School of the University of Tennessee in Knoxville, it includes classes for four days and occasional evenings every week, visits to contemporary design studios and specialized museums, viewing design works in progress, and meetings with leaders in British graphic design. Students also work on their own field-study projects.

"British graphic design has a long tradition of innovation and creativity, playing a major and influential role in graphic design internationally," note the directors. "Students will find themselves surrounded by quality design in signage, transportation, advertising, architecture, packaging, fashion, interiors and everyday objects. They will return to the United States with a different attitude, viewing their own country's design work from a new perspective."

Students are based in London and have the opportunity to visit Bath, Edinburgh, Glasgow, Oxford, Stratford-on-Avon and Stonehenge, and other cities of interest.

William Kennedy has been a member of the Department of Art's graphic design faculty since 1968, has received numerous awards for both fine art and design, and originated the graphic design history program for the University of Tennessee.

Susan Metros joined the faculty in 1984 and teaches graphic design. She established the Computer-Enhanced Design

Laboratory and Program and works internationally as a consultant to education, industry, and business on graphic design issues.

Price includes:

Airfare from Atlanta, accommodations, some meals, eight-day BritRail Pass, 30-day London Transport pass. Add tuition credit costs of $500 for a four week session.

Sample trip:

$3,000 for four weeks in London.

UNIVERSITY OF WISCONSIN/ MADISON EXTENSION

Address: **Performing Arts Study Tours**
610 Langdon Street
735 Lowell Hall
Madison WI 53703
Phone: **(608)263-6736**
Contact: **Richard Klemm**

Dozens of performing arts study tours are offered year-round by the University of Wisconsin/Madison Extension. Most tours last four to five days and are scheduled over long weekends. Each one is accompanied by a professional and experienced tour staff.

They include a weekend program in New York City with tickets to the New York Philharmonic, the New York City Ballet, the Metropolitan Opera, and a Broadway musical. There is a weekend excursion to Boston with performances by the Boston Symphony Orchestra. And there are trips to the Spoleto Festival in Charleston, South Carolina; the Santa Fe Opera and

Chamber Music Festival; and San Francisco to hear the American Conservatory Theatre and the San Francisco Symphony.

In the summer, there's a tour of Great Britain, with performances at the Edinburgh Festival in Scotland, the Abbey Theatre in Dublin, the Royal Festival Hall and the Barbican Center in London, and the Royal Shakespeare Company Theatre in Stratford-on-Avon.

Price includes:

Accommodations, some meals, best available seats to performances, educational seminars, study materials.

Sample trips:

$509 for four days in New York City.
$1,189 for eight days in London.
$2,709 for three weeks in Great Britain.

UNIVERSITY OF WISCONSIN/ MADISON OUTREACH

Address: **International Seminars**
610 Langdon Street
Madison WI 53703
Phone: **(608)263-2774**
Fax: **(608)263-2595**
Contact: **Robert H. Schacht, Director.**

Designed for "the sophisticated traveler who wants to be more than a tourist," international seminars in Morocco, Europe, Turkey, Egypt, Israel, Jordan, England, and Wales are offered by the university. They are usually led by Robert H. Schact, professor of adult education at UW/Madison. Travelers attend weekend seminars before the journey, and along the way there are briefings at embassies and by journalists, government leaders, and other local experts.

"The seminars are based on the belief that a trip abroad should be an enjoyable learning experience that helps participants better understand other people and cultures," explains Schacht.

In Morocco, participants explore the rich culture of the Arabs and the Moors which flourished in the Middle Ages and visit Rabat, Meknes, Fez, and Marrakesh; they go on to visit the cities of Seville, Cordoba, Granada, and Toledo in Spain.

In Greece and Turkey, the emphasis is on the roots of the democratic experience, with visits to Solanaceae, Delphi, Athens, Mycenae, Epidaurus, Ephesus, Troy, and Istanbul.

On the journey to Egypt, Israel, and Jordan, participants study the ancient Pharaohs; tour Tel-Aviv, Jerusalem, the Sea of Galilee and Caesarea; and spend several days in Jordan, with excursions to Petra and Jerash.

Price includes:

Airfare, accommodations in first-class hotels, most meals, excursions, transfers, fees, tips, tuition.

Sample trips:

$3,450 for 26 days in Egypt, Israel, and Jordan.
$3,995 for 22 days in Morocco and Spain.
$4,280 for 23 days in Greece and Turkey.

UNIVERSITY OF WISCONSIN/ STEVENS POINT

Address: International Programs Office
2100 Main Street
Stevens Point WI 54481
Phone: (715)346-2717
Fax: (715)346-3957
Contact: Mark Koepke, Assistant Director

"The world is like a book; he who stays at home reads only one page" declares the UW International Programs brochure, quoting Augustine.

To encourage leaving home, the university offers a range of semester and travel study programs in Britain, Poland, East and West Germany, Spain, Greece, Costa Rica, South Pacific, Australia, and China.

The excursion to Costa Rica, led by professors from the College of Natural Resources, explores cloud forests, discovers leatherback turtles, and watches active volcanoes. CNR also runs an environmental program in Poland and East and West Germany in July and August; the group researches the pollution problems in Poland and the steps taken against acid rain in the Black Forest in Germany.

The summer program on architecture and design in Britain takes students to museums, cathedrals, stately homes, galleries, and design studios and is led by Mary Ann Baird, chairperson of the Division of Fashion and Interior Design.

There's a summer bicycle tour of Europe for the athletic tourist who wants to see Europe from the seat of a bicycle, headed by Mark Koepke, a historian and an expert in biking and bike mechanics.

Semester programs in the South Pacific include three months at Dunmore Lang College in Sydney, Australia, with classes on Australian culture and civilization, natural resources and ecological issues. Study tours often include the North and South Islands of New Zealand. Other semester programs offer language, literature, culture, and history courses.

The university provides a most useful student booklet on preparing for travel abroad, with information on how to convert to the metric system, pack, budget, adjust to youth hostel life, travel by train, and cope with jet lag and homesickness.

Price includes:

Airfare from the Midwest, accommodations, most meals, transportation, field trips and tuition.

Sample trips:

$1,825 for three weeks in Costa Rica.
$1,990 for seven weeks in Poland and Germany.
$2,225 for three weeks on architecture/design, England.
$5,150 for four months in the South Pacific.

UNIVERSITY RESEARCH EXPEDITION PROGRAM

Address: **University of California**
2223 Fulton Street
Berkeley CA 94720
Phone: **(415)642-6586**
Contact: **Kay Wallis**

UREP, established in 1976, specializes in matching interested people from all walks of life with University of California scholars in need of assistance on research expeditions worldwide. No special academic or field experience is necessary to participate. Curiosity, adaptability, and willingness to share the costs and lend a helping hand are the most important qualifications.

UREP has sponsored hundreds of field teams in over 50 countries. More than 400 volunteers are involved every year assisting on research projects such as exploring the medicinal potential of chemicals produced by sponges in the South Pacific, the impact of AIDS in London, the petroglyphs and rock art of Easter Island, and the endangered butterfly species along the California coastline, among others.

In cooperation with SHARE (Science to Serve Humanity and Research for the Environment), UREP projects have expanded to help with studies of the impact of grazing yaks in Nepal, introducing native trees to the woodlands of East Africa, and creating alternative water sources for desert nomads.

Price includes:

Accommodations, all meals, tuition.
All participants make a tax-deductible donation to cover these costs. Scholarships are available.

Sample trips:

$725 for 11 days studying mule deer, High Sierra, California.
$1,245 for two weeks searching for fossils, Arizona.
$1,335 for two weeks observing festive costumes, Bolivia.

"It was the most highly concentrated two weeks of learning and cultural immersion that I've ever experienced in many years of travel," said a Californian teacher who joined an expedition to China to study the art of the Peking opera.

"A one of a kind learning experience that has sparked an interest to further investigate both the subject matter and the region," commented a woman from New Jersey, who spent two weeks excavating remains of early mammals in northern Tanzania.

UNIVERSITY STUDIES ABROAD CONSORTIUM

Address: University of Nevada
Main Library
Reno NV 89557-0093
Phone: (702)784-6569
Fax: (702)784-6010
Contact: Dr. Carmela Urza, Coordinator

Since 1983, more than 600 students from the United States and foreign universities have joined USAC programs. Participants, who must be enrolled in one of the member American universities, can register by completing an application and sending transcripts, or through the National Student Exchange. Boise State University, the University of Iowa, the Reno and Las Vegas campuses of the University of Nevada, the University of the Basque Country, the University of Pau, and the University of Turin belong to the University Studies Abroad Consortium.

Summer programs in Spain and France are available, as are semester programs in the fall, winter, and spring. In the fall and spring, there are also programs in Turin, Italy at the Scuola di Amministrazione Aziendale, a business college founded by the University of Turin in partnership with private enterprise..

A six-week summer programs emphasizes the language and culture of the Basque country, the border region between France and Spain. In Spain, students spend three days in Madrid, and then live in San Sebastian, 12 miles from the French border. There are daily language classes in Spanish, additional classes in the Basque language, and field excursions to the fishing village of Hondarribia, near Biarritz, and into the picturesque Basque countryside. Students can choose to live in a college residence, rent a room, or stay with local families.

The French summer program is held in Bayonne, an ancient city dating back to Roman times on the Atlantic coast 20 miles north of the Spanish border. The Old Quarter offers winding narrow cobblestone streets and fascinating architecture. There are daily language classes in French geared to different levels, and courses on French and Basque culture. Students live in a college residence.

Price includes:

Airfare from New York, transportation, accommodations, some meals, tuition, textbooks, excursions, insurance, International Student ID card, museums, cultural events.

Sample trips:

$3,350 for six weeks in summer, San Sebastian, Spain.
$4,850 for semester in Turin, Italy.
$5,450 for fall and winter quarters in Pau, France.

UNIVERSITY SYSTEM OF GEORGIA

Address: International Intercultural Studies Programs
100 Edgewood Avenue/Suite 1224
Atlanta GA 30303
Phone: (404)651-2450
Fax: (404)651-2028
Contact: Marion Froehlich/Susanne Thomas

"There are few experiences that can alter the way we view ourselves and the world, give us greater appreciation for our own country and culture, or help us to reassess our beliefs and values as effectively as does living in another culture," is the philosophy of the IISP, an organization of 34 state colleges and universities under the Board of Regents' auspices.

The IISP sponsors academic programs throughout the world during the summer and the academic year, maintains a resource library, and advises students and faculty interested in study, work, and travel abroad. Its programs are open to undergraduate and graduate students, high-school teachers, college faculty, and the general public.

Summer seminar programs abroad focus on particular issues. There's a course on computer science in Leicester, England; a study of education and family life in the Soviet Union; an examination of the legal basis of the European Economic Community market; comparisons of journalism in Italy and England; a tour of the World War II battlefields of Western Europe; and an analysis of the mental health and human services in Israel, among others.

Language study semesters and academic years abroad are offered at the University of Seville, Spain; at the University of Tuebingen, West Germany; and at the University of Caen, in Normandy, France. The academic year in England program is held at Queen Mary College in London and King Alfred's College in Winchester.

In summer, there are intensive French courses in Canada at Quebec's Laval University and at the universities of Tours and Dijon in France. Spanish-language courses are offered in Puebla, Mexico and Salamanca, Spain.

Price includes:

Airfare, accommodations, most meals, excursions, transportation.

Sample trips:

$2,095 for 15-day seminar in Israel.
$2,195 for six weeks studying French in Canada.
$2,995 for four weeks touring battlefields of Western Europe.

UTAH STATE UNIVERSITY

Address: USSR Travel Study Tour
Dept.of Languages and Philosophy
Logan UT 84322-0720
Phone: (801)750-1209
Contact: Dr. Kent E. Robson
Dr. Lynn R. Eliason

A tour of the Soviet Union's major Russian cities, the Baltic states, and Helsinki is offered to Utah State University students and others. The tour has run every summer since 1969.

The leaders, Dr. Robson and Dr. Eliason, are both long-time experts in the Soviet Union who speak Russian. They conduct orientation sessions before departure, provide reading lists and urge participants to take classes in Russian language, history, politics, and culture before they go.

"Last year's group visited Moscow, Leningrad, Khabarovsk, Irkutsk and Kiev in a very successful study tour," notes Dr. Robson. "New cities and republics are added in each new program to provide interest and variety."

In 1990, the program itinerary includes Leningrad, with a tour of Peter the Great's winter and summer palaces and a visit to the Hermitage Art Museum, as well as visits to Tallin, Riga, and Vilinius in the Baltic republics where Mikhail Gorbachev's new program of democratization has made the greatest strides.

Price includes:

Airfare, accommodations, all meals, transportation, excursions, theater performances.

Sample trip:

$2,875 for 17 days in the Soviet Union.

VICTOR EMANUEL NATURE TOURS

Address: **PO Box 33008**
Austin TX 78764
Phone: **(512)328-5221/(800)328-VENT**
Fax: **(512)328-2919**
Contact: **Ted Siff**

Over 100 birding and natural history tours worldwide are offered by Victor Emanuel Nature Tours, founded in 1975. About 60 percent of tour participants are repeat travelers, and some people have been on a dozen trips with the company.

"Our tours are designed to show you an impressive variety of birds and other wildlife, yet are conducted at a relaxed pace," notes president Victor Emanuel. "Our picnics in some of the world's most alluring natural areas are noteworthy in themselves. Groups are kept small to facilitate learning, better birding, and conviviality. Most of our leaders have been birding since childhood and are among the most highly renowned experts in their areas of specialization."

VENT is dedicated to conservation and supports the National Audubon Society, the World Wildlife Fund, Nature Conservancy, Conservation International, and other national and local groups. They also run birding camps for young people.

The 60 page catalog, illustrated with excellent bird drawings, offers a wide range of excursions. You can take weekend trips to Arizona, Texas, the Pacific coast, or San Diego. Longer tours from one to four weeks explore Nova Scotia and Newfoundland in Canada, Oaxaca in Mexico over Christmas, the islands of Trinidad and Tobago, Costa Rica, Guatemala, Belize, and South America.

In Europe, there's a cruise around the British Isles and a tour of Norway's coast. In Africa, participants visit Tanzania, Gabon and the Ivory Coast, Namibia and Botswana, Kenya, Madagascar, and Mauritius. You can travel through south India, take an elephant safari in the foothills of the Himalayas, visit

Borneo and the Malay Peninsula, and tour Papua New Guinea, Indonesia, and the islands of the South Pacific, as well as Australia, New Zealand, and the Antarctic. Groups travel in vans or small buses, and members are asked not to smoke in vehicles.

Price includes:

Accommodations, all meals, transportation, guide service. Airfare not included but can be booked through the company.

Sample trips:

$625 for weekend in Southeast Arizona, from Tucson.
$1,450 for 10 days in Oaxaca, Mexico, from Oaxaca.
$2,350 for two weeks in East Ecuador, from Quito.
$6,674 for a month in Australia, from Los Angeles.

V.I.P. TRAVEL

Address: **126 Milton Road**
Oak Ridge, NJ
Phone: **(201)697-7233/(800)DIAL-VIP**
Contact: **Kay Money**

"As an avocational naturalist, I use my travel company to put together two or three natural history oriented trips a year," explains Kay Money. These include whale watching on Cape Cod and sailing excursions in the Caribbean, with a focus on marine biology, aboard a windjammer.

Price includes:

Airfare, accommodations, meals, transportation.

Sample trips:

$225 for weekend whale watching in Cape Cod.
$1,500 for a week sailing in Caribbean.

VOLUNTEERS FOR PEACE

Address: International Workcamps
43 Tiffany Road
Belmont VT 05730
Phone: (802)259-2759
Fax: (802)259-2922
Contact: Peter Coldwell

"*People long for a world of plenty without the fear, violence and environmental decay experienced today. Workcamps serve as a concrete example of international cooperation, a microcosm of a world where nations join together to better the lot of humanity," states the credo of Volunteers for Peace, now affiliated with UNESCO.*

Over 800 workcamp programs are currently listed in the annual VFP International Workcamp Directory, available for $10, with projects in 33 countries; areas include the U.S., Europe, Africa, Asia, and South America. Most programs run for two to three weeks.

There's an amazing range of work opportunities. You can help reconstruct a castle in Czechoslovakia, transport mowed hay out of a nature reserve in Germany, clean a Lapp school after construction in Finland, create an exhibition hall in a small village in France, work with children in a holiday house in Ireland, research the living conditions and problems of immigrants into Italy, or maintain the National Garden of Peace in Wales. Volunteers apply for the workcamp of their choice and VFP assigns them on a first-come, first-served basis. The average age is 22.

In the United States, projects have included erosion control and trail maintenance in the White Mountains, building a wilderness trail in Alaska accessible to wheelchairs, and renovating a music school in Harlem.

Price includes:

Accommodations, meals, tuition. In effect, participants

exchange their labor on the project for food and shelter. VFP charges a registration fee. Participants pay travel costs to the site.

Sample trips:

$80 VFP fee for Western Europe and U.S.
$95 VFP for Eastern Europe.
$600 for two weeks at ecological workcamp in Russia.

"While most of the days we spent working, our nights were dedicated to dispelling the myths and false impressions about our countries," wrote a participant who built a deck and ramp at a home for the handicapped in New Jersey. "I got goosebumps as our mini-United Nations harmonized."

WARD FOUNDATION

Address: **Ward Museum of Wildfowl Art**
655 South Salisbury Boulevard
Salisbury MD 21801
Phone: **(301)742-4988/(800)742-4988**
Contact: **Donna Stalder, Public Information Coordinator**

The art of carving and painting shore birds, creating clay sculptures of different songbirds, or carving and painting a robin demands special skills. You can learn how to do it at a workshop of the Ward Foundation.

Founded in 1968 to help promote and preserve wildfowl art, the Ward Foundation sponsors the Ward Museum of Wildfowl Art, the Ward World Championship Wildfowl Carving Competition, the Ward Exhibition of Wildfowl Art, and many educational programs.

The Foundation runs summer workshops in Salisbury and Ocean City, Maryland and in the winter at Orlando, Florida. Courses include "Creating Habitats/Painting a Chickadee," "Carve, Burn and Paint a Northern Oriole," "Carve and Paint a Pintail Slick" and "The Artist in Business." Classes are taught by leading instructors from around the country.

Price includes:

Accommodation, all meals, tuition. Membership is $25 a year, and members receive a discount on fees.

Sample courses:

$150 for two-day seminar in Ocean City, Maryland.
$725 for one-week summer workshop in Maryland.
$840 for one-week winter workshop in Florida.

WESTERN ILLINOIS UNIVERSITY

Address: **Independent Travel-Study Programs**
Macomb IL 61455
Phone: **(309)298-2426**
Fax: **(309)298-2245**
Contact: **William N. Burton**

"Our Independent Travel-Study programs are designed for the independent traveler, the person traveling alone or as a member of a commercial group tour," notes a staff member of Western Illinois University. Designed for teachers, undergraduates and other adults, participants choose a study unit and earn credits for the work they do while traveling.

A selected list of 20 study units offers topics for students to choose. These include "Historic Landscapes" which requires participants to find, examine and interpret sites with physical reminders of the past. "Music and Society" needs an analysis of some aspect of music, from street singers to grand opera, from a composer's studio to a museum collection of musical instruments. "Rural Land Use Patterns" demands on-site research into field size and shape, fencing, crops, patterns of cultivation, and agricultural technology. A program on "Literary Landscapes" sends students out to examine the countryside and environment described in the works of selected authors.

Participants choose their independent travel-study abroad or in the United States, or take a group tour. They are required to prepare a bibliography, attend an orientation session, create a study outline, and write a report of their findings.

Price includes:
Participants choose independent trips.

WESTERN MICHIGAN UNIVERSITY

Address: **Office of International Affairs**
2090 Friedmann Hall
Kalamazoo MI 49008-5011
Phone: **(616)387-3951**
Fax: **(616)387-3962**
Contact: **Dr. Howard Dooley, Assistant Dean, International Affairs**

One of the most popular of WMU's travel study programs abroad is the Oxford Seminar Program at Oxford University, England, which takes place in odd-numbered years (1991, 1993, 1995 are next). Students live in one of Oxford University's 33 historic colleges and attend lectures on literature, history, and culture, as well as taking trips to London, Scotland, Wales, Stratford-on-Avon, and Stonehenge. A 10-day tour of Europe can be added to the Seminar.

In even-numbered years (1990, 1992, 1994), WMU offers a Grand Tour of Europe, with a month of summer travel through Holland, France, Switzerland, Italy, Austria, and Germany. There's also a 10-day trip to London, including a backstage theater tour and tickets to two shows.

The WMU summer programs travel to Mexico, Europe, Africa, Egypt, and the Soviet Union. The trip to the Soviet Union is led by Dr. Jim Butterfield, professor of political science at WMU, an expert on Soviet life, history, culture, and politics who also speaks fluent Russian. Participants visit Moscow, Leningrad, Tbilisi in Georgia, and Riga in Latvia, and meet with Russian students to discuss the new glasnost, nuclear arms, the environment, and world peace.

Price includes:

Airfare, accommodations, most meals, day tours, excursions, tuition, administrative expenses.

Sample trips:

$2,499 for 15 days in the Soviet Union.
$2,889 for 30 days on Grand Tour of Europe.
$3,149 for month at Oxford University, England.
$3,295 for 18 days in East Africa.

WESTERN RIVER EXPEDITIONS

Address: 7258 Racquet Club Drive
Salt Lake City UT 84121
Phone: (801)942-6669/(800)453-7450
Fax: (801)942-8514
Contact: Darla M. Roberts

Since 1955, Western River Expeditions, the largest rafting vacation company in the United States, has taken thousands of guests down rivers in Utah, Arizona, and Colorado. They promise that even sedentary souls with no previous wilderness experience can discover how to hurtle through foaming rapids, drift along lazily in the desert sun, hike cool canyons, splash in side streams and waterfalls, and sleep under the stars.

The company offers motor, paddle, and oar expeditions in the Green River wilderness, down the wild water of Westwater and Cataract Canyons on the Colorado, and through the Grand Canyon. On some trips, you ride "J-rig" rafts, patented and designed by Western River Expeditions. These large, power-driven rubber craft are 37 feet long, 18 feet wide, and extremely sturdy.

Videos of raft rides through the Grand Canyon, Cataract Canyon, and down the Green River are available.

Price includes:

Camping gear, all meals, boats, guides, transportation to and from river.

Sample trips:

$395 for three days on Westwater, Colorado River.
$635 for four or five days on Green River; Tavaputs Ranch option available..
$1,265 for six days through Grand Canyon, Colorado River.

WESTERN WASHINGTON UNIVERSITY

Address: **Mongolian Summer Program**
Center for East Asian Studies
Bellingham WA 98225
Phone: **(206)676-3041**
Contact: **Professor Henry G. Schwarz, Director**

An intensive course in the Mongolian language is part of the experience offered by Western Washington University's Mongolian summer program. Students travel to China and follow a specially prepared curriculum of conversation, grammar, reading and drill for 8 weeks in Mongolia.

Classes are held five days a week, from 8 to 11 in the mornings, and from 3 to 5 in the afternoons, a total of 160 hours of classroom instruction. The course is considered the equivalent of a one-year semi-intensive course in the language. Those who complete it receive a certificate from Inner Mongolia University.

Classes take place at the Inner Mongolia University in Hohhot, capital of the Inner Mongolian Autonomous Region of China. Students live and eat in a recently completed guest house on the campus. There are excursions to famous cultural centers in and around Hohhot, visits to Mongolian herding areas, and showings of Mongolian movies and television programs. Those who want may stay longer to travel to other parts of the country.

Before going, students are expected to take the basic survey course on Mongolian society and culture at Western Washington University or should read about it independently.

Professor Schwarz notes that "prices of everyday goods in Hohhot are extremely low by American standards, and our cost is lower than that of any other summer program in China of comparable length and content."

Price includes:

Airfare, accommodations, meals, tuition, materials, cultural events, excursions.

Sample trip:

$2,750 for eight weeks in Hohhot, China.

WILDERNESS SOCIETY

Address: **Advocates for Wilderness Trips**
900 17th Street, NW
Washington DC 20006
Phone: **(202)833-2300**
Contact: **Ali F. Phillips, Trips Coordinator**

Trips to explore the wilderness areas in America are part of the educational work of the Wilderness Society. Members who contribute $1,000 or more can participate as an Advocate for Wilderness.

"Our trips are small, usually no more than 12 guests," noted Ali Phillips, "and take you to the natural areas we are struggling to save. They are designed for everyone, from the inexperienced to the hardy hiker."

Regions visited include the National Wildlife Refuges in southern Texas for bird watching, Cumberland National Seashore in Georgia to explore its beaches and forests, and Alaska's Arctic National Wildlife Refuge for rafting and hiking. There are also horse-packing trips in southwest Virginia, hiking in Maine's northern woods, and snorkeling in the Florida Keys, among others. Some trips stay in comfortable lodges, while others offer back-country camping.

Price includes:

Accommodations, meals, transportation, guides, charters, gratuities.

Sample trips:

$490 for three days exploring Everglades in Florida.
$845 for five days bird watching in southern Texas.
$1,190 for six days cross-country skiing in Yellowstone.
$2,500 for 10 days in Alaska's Arctic Refuge.

WILD HORIZONS EXPEDITIONS

Address: **West Fork Road**
Darby MT 59829
Phone: **(406)821-3747**
Contact: **Howie Wolke**

"In wildness is the preservation of the world," wrote Henry Thoreau more than a century ago.

A respect for the spectacular beauty of the remaining rugged wilderness areas of the west inspires Wild Horizons Expeditions. The company offers backpack trips for adults and teens, as well as custom and family trips designed for specific groups. The guides are excellent naturalists and skilled in low-impact hiking and camping techniques. WHE was founded in 1978 and is a licensed guide and outfitter with the U.S. Forest Service, the National Park Service, and the U.S. Fish and Wildlife Service.

In Canyonlands National Park, participants learn about the natural history of Southern Utah's Red Rock Canyon country, with its spectacular rock formations, canyon walls, arches, cool desert streams, and the wildlife of desert bighorns, pumas, bobcats, coyotes, and golden eagles.

An expedition into Yellowstone National Park examines the effects of the 1988 fires and the ecosystems of the Rockies, where the forest floor is already a carpet of grass, flowers and lodgepole pine seedlings, and the meadows are greener than ever. Bison, elk, mules, deer, grizzly bears, and birds abound.

And in Montana, travelers stay on Wild Horizons property in the Bitterroot Range for a seminar on the ecology of the northern Rocky Mountains and then go backpacking into the Wild River of No Return Wilderness.

"We generally limit each expedition to eight participants," states Howie Wolke, president and founder of the company. He sets a moderate pace, covering about six miles a day, with at least one rest day "so folks can explore, fish, day hike, or just lie back and soak up the rays of the sun."

Price includes:

Accommodations, all meals, equipment, trip planning, fees, transportation.

Sample trips:

$550 for six days in Canyonland National Park, Utah.
$595 for seven days in Absoraka Range, Wyoming.
$695 for eight days in Sonoran Desert, Arizona.

WILDLANDS STUDIES

Address: **San Francisco State University**
3 Mosswood Circle
Cazadero CA 95421
Phone: **(707)632-5665**
Contact: **Crandall and Marcene Bay**

This project welcomes volunteers willing to serve as field associates to scientific environmental research teams working in Alaska, North Carolina, Wyoming, California, Montana, Hawaii, Utah, China, Nepal, and Canada on wildland ecological problems.

"Field work sometimes means long days and uphill trails in not always ideal weather," explained Crandall Bay, director of Wildland Studies. "At times, research can be frustrating, repetitious, or just plain hard work. But it is also a rare and fascinating opportunity to explore our wildlands first hand."

In Alaska, the team explores the Kennicott Glacier, observing the behavior of grizzly bears, black bears, and moose. There are climbs into alpine regions to see how plants adapt to the sub-Arctic atmosphere and to note geologic evidence showing the Wrangell Mountains terrain migrated from the South Pacific.

In Idaho and Wyoming, researchers examine the natural behavior of animals and birds: the nesting behavior of the bald eagle in the Snake River Canyon, the social relationships among mountain goats in the peaks of the Snake River range, and how lambs play among Bighorn sheep in the Teton Mountain Range.

On the border of British Columbia and Montana, a team studies the status and behavior of wolves, who roamed the Rocky Mountains and are now returning there from Canada. And in Utah, a team studies the canyons of the Colorado Plateau.

Price includes:

Project fee. Participants also pay $40 application fee, share costs of food and on-site transportation, provide their own backpacking equipment.

Sample trips:

$385 for three weeks on red wolf project, North Carolina.
$385 for two weeks on California bobcat Project.
$760 for six weeks in Glacier National Park, Montana.

After a summer exploring Montana's Gallatin wildlands, one participant commented: "The instructors gave their whole selves to teaching us. Their implicit attitude toward the wilderness and their around-the-clock willingness and availability for engaged discussion made this course on of the most enriching learning experiences I've ever had."

WOLF TRAP ASSOCIATES

Address: **Wolf Trap Farm Park for the Performing Arts**
1551 Trap Road
Vienna VA 22182
Phone: **(703)255-1940**
Fax: **(703)255-1896**
Contact: **Heidi Klein**

Wolf Trap Farm was created when the gift of 100 acres of Virginia farmland and funds to build an arts center in Vienna was accepted by an act of Congress in 1966.

This unique indoor/outdoor theater presents opera, dance, jazz, symphony, musical theater and other productions selected by its foundation members. The center offers year-round educational programs related to the arts.

Wolf Trap Associates support the center by volunteering, contributing, and extending community support and can join the educational travel tours. These include a weekend in Bucks County, Pennsylvania to visit museums; a weekend in New York with theater performances and visits to art galleries; and a week in London attending theater and concerts.

Price includes:

Accommodations, some meals, transportation, activities, events, guide.

Sample trips:

$35 for one-day trip to Washington, DC.
$225 for weekend in Bucks County, PA.
$640 for weekend in New York City.

WORLD WILDLIFE FUND

Address: **1250 24th Street NW**
Washington DC 20037
Phone: **(202)778-9683**
Fax: **(202)293-9211**
Contact: **Candra Currie**

Members of the World Wildlife Fund explore the great natural wonders of the world—tropical rain forests, deserts, savanna lands, snow-capped Himalayan mountains, volcanic craters, highland lakes, tropical beaches, and coral reefs. Trips are headed by natural history experts and include visits to WWF project sites and discussions with field staff and local conservation leaders.

On the WWF East African safari, participants visit outstanding national parks and reserves in Kenya and Tanzania. They tour the vast Serengeti Plain, where countless thousands of wildebeest and zebras wander, and the Masai Mara with its elephant families, lions, hippos, and crocodiles.

The Galapagos and Ecuador expedition sails among the islands to see blue-footed boobies, land and sea iguanas, and miniature penguins. Other trips travel through Brazil's Amazonia National Park, Madagascar's nature reserves with their protected lemurs and reptiles, Borneo and Indonesia, Argentina, Thailand and Nepal.

Price includes:

Accommodations, most meals, air and land transportation, tips, leadership.

Sample trips:

$2,490 for 14 days in Costa Rica; from Miami.
$3,490 for 13 days in the Galapagos Islands.
$5,800 for 21-day Kenya and Tanzania safari.

"The extraordinarily high degree of professional knowledge and enthusiasm as well as the very pleasant personalities of our leaders added greatly to the trip," commented a participant on the trip to Madagascar.

"One of the most interesting and informative trips I have had," noted a WWF traveler to Brazil.

YELLOWSTONE INSTITUTE

Address: Yellowstone Association
Box 117
Yellowstone Natl Park, WY 82190
Phone: June-Aug (307)344-7749
Sept-May (208)236-2207
Contact: Don Streubel,
Yellowstone Association Director
Park Visitor Services: (307)344-7381

The wonders of Yellowstone Park in Wyoming with its snow-covered mountains, waterfalls, acres of flower-covered fields, and steaming hot springs are unequalled. For visitors eager to learn more about this unique environment, there are courses on the history, ecology, and wildlife of the Park offered by the Yellowstone Institute from June to September.

The Institute is organized by the Yellowstone Association, a non-profit organization founded in 1933 to support educational, historical, and scientific programs for the benefit of Yellowstone National Park and its visitors.

Every summer there are seminars on a range of topics; titles include "Wildflowers of the High Country," "Yellowstone's Night Skies," "Lakes of Yellowstone by Canoe," "Flyfishing the Catch and Release Way," "Geysers, Mudpots and Hot Springs" and "Bears: Folklore and Biology," among dozens of courses. Most last a few days and take place in Yellowstone.

The teachers include Tom McBride, who leads the seminar on "Wildlife Photography in Yellowstone" and was Photographer of the Year of the Montana Professional Photographers Association and is a still photographer for the Library of Congress. Jeanne M. Eder, a member of the Sioux tribe and assistant professor of Native American studies at Eastern Montana College, teaches "Indian Use of Yellowstone." Several courses on the effects of the 1988 fires in the park show its remarkable recovery.

Some courses are held in the Institute's log-cabin facility, where participants live in wooden cabins without plumbing, heating, or electricity—described as "indoor camping"—and bring their own food. Cooking is done in the communal kitchen with stove, utensils and refrigerator, but space is limited. There are campgrounds and hotels in the park and several motels outside the park.

Most of the courses take students outdoors hiking, horsepacking, camping, canoeing and on llama treks.

Price includes:

Tuition only for courses held at Institute; tuition, meals and lodging on excursions.

Sample courses:

$75 for two-day course on elk in Yellowstone.
$295 for five-day canoe trip across Lewis and Shoshone Lakes.
$360 for five-day llama trek on Shoshone Lake Trail.

YOSEMITE MOUNTAINEERING SCHOOL AND GUIDE SERVICE

Address: **Yosemite CA 95389**
Phone: **(209)372-1244**
Contact: **Bruce Brossman**

Set in the heart of Yosemite National Park in California, this school, authorized by the National Park Service, Department of the Interior, offers instruction in rock climbing, low-impact back-packing and camping during the summer and in cross-country skiing, skating, snow-shoeing, and ski-touring during the winter.

The summer backpacking trips cater to beginners as well as to more experienced hikers and climbers. As a leader explained: "We demonstrate how to use various types of backpacking equipment such as stoves, tents, fishing tackle, clothing, etc."

Participants learn to find their way with map and compass, store food correctly, build emergency shelters, make a fire, and develop skills for survival in adverse weather conditions.

In winter, snow sports take over. Yosemite National Park has 350 miles of trails for skiing and snowshoeing. Guides lead overnight ski trips to Glacier Point, where guests bunk in the Glacier Point hut. There's an overnight snow-camping trip on which participants learn to build a snow shelter, prepare food, and practice basic survival skills. And from a base camp in Tuolumne Meadows, there's a six-day ski expedition across the Sierra Nevada Mountains.

Price includes:

Accommodations, breakfast, dinner, instruction. All backpacking and ski equipment can be rented.

Sample trips:

Mountaineering:

$100 for introduction to backpacking.
$180 for 4-day backpacking and climbing trip.

Skiing:

$130 for overnight hut ski trip.
$350 for six-day ski trip.

INDEX

ORDER FORM

NAME..

ADDRESS...

....

CITY..

STATE....................ZIP.................

PHONE...(.........)..........................

PRICE: $23.95 per copy, plus $2.05 for shipping.
TOTAL: $26.00

Please send .... copy/ies TRAVEL AND LEARN

Enclosed is my check for $...................
made payable to: BLUE PENGUIN PUBLICATIONS

Send to: Blue Penguin/Sales
147 Sylvan Avenue, Leonia NJ 07605.

ALL ORDERS MUST BE PREPAID.

Please allow 4 to 6 weeks for delivery.

Thank you.